DEAR BELLA...

...This Family Is F**ked

Azaria Faver

This book is dedicated to Steffs mum, who - regardless of what went on between me and him - always treated me like one of her own. And I will never forget that.
Thank you J xx

FOREWORD

As most people are aware, in the last year I have made some drastic changes for myself and my wee family, and have had to take myself out of a very toxic family environment.
I hope this book gives people an insight into why I've made the decisions I've made as of late.

Thanks

Azaria

INTRODUCTION

Dear Bella...

I was classed as a gifted child before all of this shit.

When I was 4, I was reading Shakespeare fluently. When I was 12, I sat the MENSA exam at Glasgow Caledonian University, ran out of time during the second half which affected my score – I wasn't accepted into the high IQ society at 12 years old because my score suggested my IQ was higher than only 96% of the UK population; in order to be accepted your IQ had to be higher than 98%.

I never once studied at school, rarely listened to the teachers and only done homework a handful of times throughout my time there. And yet I flew through my exams, leaving school with high grades at 16.
The plan for me was to do my Highers, before doing biology at university, and then moving on to pathology, the goal being I eventually qualified as a forensic pathologist.

It's weird because you're gifted, but not really. You are constantly placed on a pedestal, you are constantly expected to do things other children aren't capable of, when you really just want to be doing the same shit as the other kids.

People just assumed things about me. They assumed that I LOVED reading, when I actually fucking hate reading. Ironic, eh?
The author that hates reading. But I fucking do.

So, every Christmas, I would get books. I remember getting the first Harry Potter book, it was a big deal. I read a couple of pages and ended up destroying the rest with brightly coloured scribbles.

Your great-granny, my Granny Faver, gave me a book when I was 5, and it was the only book I truly enjoyed reading. I cherished it.

It was about Tutankhamun. It was an old book; the pages were almost brown with nicotine. I think it belonged to your great-auntie when she was younger, as her name was in the front. I read that book from back to front, I would sit and teach myself how to pronounce each word in that book.

And, it created a topic that me and your granddad could speak about, as he loved history, his dream was to be an archaeologist, he spoke to me often about Egypt. Right up until I started taking smack.

One of my favourite stories is the story of Ra and Apophis, and your granddad sat and told me it one night when we were sitting in his car, in a field in East Lothian, watching the moon. It's always stuck with me.

Ra was one of the most important Gods of Egypt. He was the God of the sun, order and the sky. He created all forms of life. The Egyptians' believed Ra was the sun, therefore they worshipped him.

When Ra was born, his discarded umbilical cord formed into his darker side – Apep, who became known as Apophis. He formed into a giant snake, and became the God of chaos in the world.

When the sun, Ra, went down at night, he would climb into his solar boats, and travel through the night, which was the literal underworld, accompanied by other gods. He would eat the monsters of the underworld to attain eternal power, and spit them back out into the sky at the end of his journey, giving the sky a red hue in the morning.

But Apophis was a total fucking dick, the fucker was relentless. The giant serpent would spend every night trying to kill Ra. Sometimes he would consume the solar boat and gods whole, other times he would freeze them with a hypnotic stare. He would wait at the start of the underworld at sundown, and lurk around the end of the underworld first thing in the morning. When I say he was relentless, I fucking mean it – he was a total arsehole of a god.

Sometimes I felt like Ra. I felt like I was constantly being accosted by the chaotic god that is Heroin.

Sometimes I would think I'd have escaped it, and then boom – it would consume me whole.

Other times it would leave me and my entire life frozen with a hypnotic stare. Whilst other peoples lives continued on, I was trapped in a suspended animation controlled by addiction. It didn't have to consume me whole, all it had to do was trap me with that fucking stare, and I would destroy myself on its behalf.

Some parts of my life, things would be great during the day – I often fooled people into thinking I was clean. But as soon as I finished work, and closed the family café, I would jump on my solar boat, and into the underworld. I would spend the night travelling through the underworld, trying to fight my addiction, and failing. But by the morning, I would be reborn.

But I've also felt like Apophis.
I've felt like I am the god of chaos, that leaves trails of destruction wherever I go. I've felt like I'm the one that consumes other people, desperately trying to block their light just so I can feel powerful. I've felt like the physical embodiment of chaos, clawing at the ankles of people trying to escape in their own solar boats, trying to drag them back down into the pit of addiction with me. Because it's fucking lonely down there.

But I am Azaria, and I am your Mum, and I am both the creator of life, and the embodiment of chaos.
And that fight will always swirl around inside of my chest. I wish it ended long ago; I wish I didn't have any material to write more than 1 book.

But please, always know, that no matter who I am, I will always use the force of the sun, and the force of chaos, to protect you.

CHAPTER 1

Life doesn't feel real.

I know we all lose our parents some day, but I didn't feel like I would lose my Dad at 18.

He was perfectly fucking healthy when I left home. He never, ever smoked. He only ever had a can of Newcastle Brown Ale every now and again. How does someone fall so, so unwell and die so quickly? How does that even happen?

And then there's people like me, pumping myself full of every dangerous substance known to man, walking around without a care in the world.

I still can't believe this shit; I just want my fucking Dad. I'm still at Mums, but it's very clear I'm not entirely welcome here.

Apparently when she reported me missing last year, when the policewoman seen my bedroom, she asked my Mum "why the Hell would any 17 year old girl want to live out on the streets when she could be living here?".

I'll tell you why – because I'm not welcome, and never have been. I don't know if she realises the obstacles she puts in my way when it comes to recovery. And don't even get me started on her piece of shit husband.

Bella, a wee while ago your Gran told me that your Stepdad isn't your Stepdad – he's just my partner. According to her, he would only be a Stepdad if your biological Dad died, which is nonsense, as that usage fell out of use in the early 1800s. Legally, a Stepdad is a man that is in a relationship with the mother - that is the literal definition in the Oxford dictionary, and in Scottish/British law.

However, you need to take into account, that mentality is totally normal for your grandmother, as it was clear that man only wanted a relationship with her and nothing to do with me or your uncle. If he did what most people did nowadays, and stepped up as a father figure, maybe he wouldn't have asked me to suck his dick.

And if your Granny looked at him as more than just "her husband", maybe she wouldn't have taken him back after she found out he asked me to suck his dick.

Bella, William and I never, ever want you to feel unloved. Even if your dad was still involved, William would still love and treat you like his own, because neither of us ever want you to feel uncomfortable in YOUR own house. I know that, at the moment, you still struggle accepting him, you still struggle with a lot, which is natural, but that man will never ever come before you.

You will always know where home is.

You will always feel where home is.

It's taken me 2 days, but I have finally finished the eulogy for dads funeral. I don't often struggle with writing, but this eulogy was a nightmare. After hours of staring at a blank word processor, and researching various poems and funeral speeches online, I eventually turned the desktop computer off and pulled out some paper.

And as soon as the tip of the biro touched the paper, it just came out naturally. So, instead of writing a typical funeral speech, I've written a letter direct to dad. I've poured everything into it, and I think I cried the entire time, but it's beautiful, and it's from the heart. And I know he would appreciate everything I've said.

I jump off my bed and fire downstairs with the letter in hand, proud as punch. It's just perfect, it's really, really perfect. He would love it and I know everyone at the funeral will feel the emotion in every word.

Mums sitting in the living area with her friend, my Auntie D, at the other side of the huge kitchen. I immediately tell them that I've finished writing the eulogy, and explain that I've written a letter to dad instead. They seem intrigued and pleased at the idea, and I proudly hand the letter to my mum first.

For five minutes, I stand watching her, my heart sinking as I watch her eyes move across and down each line, screwing her face up occasionally. When she gets to the end, the snaps the letter across to my Auntie D, and begins "Well..."

"Well, what?" I'm stunned, and I don't even know what she's got to say yet.

"WELL," She begins again, "it's nice, but that part where you've written that he was the ONLY person that's been there for you, that's a load of rubbish."

She starts reeling off a list of how she has been there for me, and everything she states is material.

How she is the one that went out working X number of hours, whilst my dad never paid child support.
How she is the one that picked up the phone on the night I came home, not my dad (who was dying of terminal cancer, which was a big part of him wanting nothing to do with me for the first couple of weeks I came back).
How it was her that came with me to social work appointments.

But... That's a parents job. And completely irrelevant for the way I stated my dad supported me in the letter. It was clear I meant emotional support.

I remember breaking down one night, when I was 15, on his bathroom floor. He got down on that floor beside me and held me for 2 hours, before carrying me through to bed.

I remember breaking down during a core group meeting with my social worker, because I didn't have any friends. It was the social worker that held my hand as mum got out of her chair, walked out of the office and drove home.

I remember my dad seeing my self-harm scars on my arm, he again held me as I sat sobbing into his chest, telling him I didn't know why I had a compulsion to harm myself.

I remember my mum seeing my self-harm scars, and scoffing, before telling me to stop attention seeking. Granted, she took me to the doctors, so I could get someone to speak to.

But I wanted to speak to her, I wanted to be able to speak to my mum.

But the only person it seemed she was interested in speaking to was her husband.

I pray to God you don't ever feel that way about me, Bella.

Auntie D finishes the letter, and clearly trying to diffuse the situation, starts talking about how nice the letter is. But that doesn't stop my mother, who continues on for another 5 minutes about everything she's done for me.

Anything I do for you, as a parent, will never be held against you.
The "what about everything I've done for you!?" attitude as a parent is fucking disgusting.
Aye, I've fed you. Clothed you. Looked after you when you're sick. Put a roof over your head. When you've been in trouble, I've been there, when you've been upset, I've been there. And I always will be, there is no age limit, there is no "as soon as you 18 you're on your own".
All of those things are the basics of parenting, and it will never be held against you.
Don't get me wrong, I often drill into you the importance of appreciating what you have, such as nice clothes, nice toys, nice food – but I just want you to appreciate that you get the "finer" things in life.
Some days we eat Heinz beans, and other days we eat ASDA JUST ESSENTIALS beans. I want you to appreciate the times we eat the better quality Heinz beans – not the fact we're eating beans. The beans will always be there, because as a parent it's my responsibility to feed you.
I will never make you feel bad about that – you didn't ask to be born.

I force a wee smile at Auntie D, but the anger inside of me is clawing its way up my throat, so I take the letter back, tell mum I'll change that line, and go back upstairs.

And cry. I cry so fucking hard, I'm doing that silent screaming thing into my pillow, which is now drenched in tears.

I can't believe she has just made the Eulogy for my dad about her. I just can't believe it.

Dad, I really fucking need you right now man this isn't funny.
I can't go through this shite without you.

Yes, I did change the line in the eulogy, to include her.
I'm still angry at myself for doing it.

CHAPTER 2

<u>February 19th 2010</u>
<u>I don't want to do this; I don't think I can. I honestly don't know if</u>
<u>I can go to my dads funeral.</u>

But it's too late now because I'm sitting in the funeral car with my brother, Rose, and her adult children. It's a really weird silence, each person is visibly awkward. And in the awkward chit-chat, we somehow get onto the subject of names, as in what our parents would've named us had they not given us our names.

"Dad wanted to call me Daisa, like Daisy, but with an 'ah' at the end," they look at me confused, "so my name would be Daisa Faver. Like, daes a favour?"

My brother bursts out laughing beside me, "it's like the ultimate dad joke."

We're all laughing really hard, it doesn't feel like we're on our way to a funeral.

Roses daughter pipes up, "if I was born a girl I was going to be called…"

Her brother reminds her she was born a girl, and we all start laughing again.

This is weird because it genuinely doesn't feel like we are about to say goodbye to my dad, it feels like we're sharing a taxi home after a night in the pub.

And then we pull into Mortonhall crematorium, and each one of us immediately falls silent. As soon as we turn in, and see a crowd of people wearing black in the distance, I start shaking. I can see my little brothers knuckles turning white, I can't look at him, it'll send me over the fucking edge.

The car pulls in, we step out, and I exhale the biggest sigh of relief when my brother walks in the opposite direction, to the back of the car, as he is one of the pall bearers.
I can't look at him.

I'm standing in a black dress and heels, swaying a bit because I honestly feel like this is a simulation. I'm only brought back to earth when Rose takes my hand. I look up and suddenly, I realise my worst nightmare has become reality – there is a sea of women staring back at me.

Girlfriends.

Not just girlfriends – fiancées, also. Three, to be exact.

And Rose, his wife of 48 hours.

And ex-girlfriends.

And "friends" that were women, but clearly didn't want their husbands knowing about my dad.

Bella this all sounds like total bullshit and most people will read this and think "aye no bother". Aye, no fucking bother. Ask your uncle, your granny, his wife! Apparently, he was going to be marrying his 3 fiancées on Inchcombe Island, on the same month, on the same year. Your grandad loved women. And he loved the thrill of living multiple lives. Unfortunately, this led to a lot of people being hurt over the span of his life.

I'm shaking really hard now, I'm sitting at the front next to rose, but there's a gap in between us for my brother. Out of the corner of my eye, I see other people looking back, so I automatically look back with them. It's the biggest mistake I could make – I lock eyes with my brother, who is at the front, carrying the coffin in. He's bright red and doing a really bad job of keeping the hysterics locked inside himself, I can see him trying to control his violent shaking and doing that rapid inhale thing you do when you're trying not to cry. I don't know if he's going to make it down the aisle, but he does.

I don't know why I'm not crying. I want to, but I can't.

When the coffin is laid down, he sits between me & rose. The service begins, and I don't register a single word the humanitarian says, it's not until he says my name, and prompts me to get up, that I come back down to earth for the second time today.

I could really do with a fucking bag right now.

I get up and stand at the altar, with the few sheets of notepad paper in front of me. I don't know if I can just start speaking, or if I have to lean into the microphone, I don't know what the protocol here is, I need fucking help.

Someone help me, please.

The only person I can face looking at is the humanitarian, and he motions for me to begin.

"Well dad," I start, "I always told you I would get the last word…"

And for just over five minutes I stand there, choking periodically, reading every word, and meaning every word. When I get to the end and say goodbye, I look at the coffin.

That's it.

Can't fucking do this. Nope.

I step down from the altar, and start walking, intent on leaving. But as I approach the first row, and I see my brother sitting there, still sobbing, I turn and sit back down.

I hold his hand.

And we cry together.

CHAPTER 3

I couldn't do it. I couldn't stay away.

The funeral ended about 6 hours ago, and now, here I am, back smoking heroin with Steff. We're in some guys flat, he's in prison and the door was locked – Steff booted it in. His name is Ritchie, he's just another addict, known schizophrenic, and very vulnerable. Random people using his flat as Scottish opium den is the norm – whether he's in prison or not.

I can't stop crying, and he's sitting next to me, stroking my hair and holding me. I knew he loved me, if he didn't, he wouldn't be here now, comforting me.

There's no comfort at "home", and there never will be – I've accepted that. It's already been made very clear to me that now the funeral is over and done with, that I need to get a job pronto. As in, within the next few days. Just get on with it.

So, I've done what I always do – went looking for comfort elsewhere.
And my comfort is heroin.

Bella, no matter what you experience in life, I will always be a source of comfort for you. There is no time limit on grief, or recovery from shitty experiences. Putting on a brave face, and continuing on with lifes other pressures as if nothing has happened, will just make the healing process longer and harder. I will never pressure you into "just getting over" things, never. Because that pressure often damaged me as much as the original traumatic experience.

Steff passes me the tooter, and I lean forward over the tinfoil as he starts burning it from underneath. Oh my god, this shite still tastes just as disgusting as I remember. Over the past few weeks being clean, I kinda forgot how rancid this shit tastes. I start heaving, and before the vomit reaches the threshold that is my mouth, I manage to shoot through to the bathroom. As soon as I swing the door open, I swing my jaws open as well and unleash liquid hell all over the toilet. The lid was closed, for fuck sake.

As soon as the sick is out of my system, it's like the heroin kicks in tenfold, and I become unsteady on my feet. Staring at the mess my stomach has just created, I forget to bend my knee somehow and fall sideways, only being stopped by the wall.

Fuck it.

I turn from my shoulder on to my back, and slide down the wall, next to the vomit covered toilet. I look at my hands, they're black – tinfoil marks.

I break down again.

I can't believe I'm back doing this, what the fuck is wrong with me?
WHAT THE FUCK IS WRONG WITH ME FOR FUCK SAKE???

I just want my dad.

CHAPTER 4

It's been a week since the funeral, and the relapse. I stayed the night with Steff that night, and came home in the morning. I haven't seen him since; I really do want to stay away. I don't want to go back to the smack, I shouldn't have fucking done it again, why the fuck did I do that? What the fuck is wrong with me?

I literally stood and gave that speech at dads' funeral, and I DID mean every word. So why did I still go out, meet Steff, and get wasted on Kit?

You know what, fuck it. I can't sit feeling pure guilty because all it's doing is making me feel bad and want to go back out. And anytime I tell someone this, they have a go at me for feeling that way.

Why should I feel this way? I'm living in a 6-bedroom new build home, back with my family. I should appreciate this, and I do.

But... I don't feel like it's my home. My family doesn't feel like my family, with the exception of my little brother. I feel like I live with my brother, and some woman and her husband.

Bella, you're in Primary 1 now. This morning when I was walking you to school, I told you "I love you so much, more than anything else. I love you more than William, you always come before him,". You know what your reply was? "You tell me that every day, mum,".
And it suddenly hit me, that yes – I do. I am so overly paranoid about you feeling like you come after my partner, that every single day I feel the need to remind you that you come first. You probably find it a bit strange, but I will never stop verbalising my love for you.

You will always come first.

I'm sitting in my bedroom with a piece of paper in front of me, scribbling down my personal information, and everything else you put into a CV. Obviously, I've basically no work history, but I'm only 18, plus my mums' friend (who owns a salon), is letting me use her as a reference for the past 2 years, which is super helpful. Still, the entire country is still reeling from the effects of the 2008 recession, and getting a job right now… Trust me, it's fucking hard. My mum and her idiot husband have no idea how hard it is, actually, because they've always been in long term employment. They haven't had to try and get a job ASAP, with essentially no work experience, a history of heroin addiction, and escalating mental health issues.

They think I'm just lazy, and making all of the excuses under the sun to not find work, but that's not true. I really am fucking trying. But there's nothing.

Walking downstairs, I read over everything I've written and I'm fairly confident it'll get me a few interviews, at the very least. All I need to do is type it up – I can't hand in a hand-written CV to an employer, it's 2010.

"Mum," I walk into the kitchen, where she's standing ironing, "can I use your computer? It's just to type up and print my CV,".
"No," She responds, abruptly.

I… Didn't expect that response. She's the one that's banging on to me about getting a job. I don't understand why she won't allow me. The computer isn't in use right now. She's never really had an issue before.

"But, it's just to write my CV…" I begin explaining, before being swiftly cut off.

"Azaria, I said NO,"

I can feel the lump in my throat increasing in size by the second, "then how the fuck am I supposed to get a job without a proper CV???"

She doesn't reply, as she continues to iron.

"Mum, come on, I need to write this CV," I'm starting to plead. I just want to get a fucking job, "How can I get a job without a CV!?"

"Go to the careers centre,"

Oh, my fucking god. She's honestly expecting me to spend half an hour trekking to the careers centre, in the town next to ours, and I can guarantee she will not give me the bus fares.
There's a perfectly good computer in the dining room, that she normally lets me use!

Like an uppercut, I'm smashed with the reality that, no matter what I do, she's not going to allow me to use the computer to do my CV.

I turn, and as I open the kitchen door, to go back upstairs to cry, my brother appears.

"Mum," he smiles, unaware of the conversation he's walked into, "can I use your computer to play Minecraft?"

She chirps up, "No bother son,"

She puts the iron down, walks into the dining room, and enters her password to open up the computer.

I stand there, astonished. Physically unable to speak.

I can't fucking believe this. I can't believe she's just fucking done that.

Oh, my fucking God!!!!!!!!!!!!!!

AHHHHHHHHHHHHHHHHHHHHH

AND SHE WONDERS WHY I DON'T WANT TO BE HERE?
FUCK MY NICELY DECORATED BEDROOM. FUCK THE NICE CLOTHES. FUCK THE MARKS & SPENCER FOOD. FUCK IT ALL!

I just want Steff.

CHAPTER 5

Fuck.

I'm back here again, at Ritchies flat, with Steff, smoking a score bag. I started a claim for jobseekers' allowance, £53 a week. But it takes a couple of weeks to get your first payment whilst they set up your claim, so I phoned for a crisis loan.

It's a piece of piss. You phone them for free, sit on hold for 40 minutes listening to Vivaldis' Le Quattro Stagioni – spring, you just spiel the usual bullshit – I have no money, I've only got 50 pence left in the electric, and that's emergency, nothing in gas. No food. Nothing. I am completely destitute until my claim is processed in two weeks. And ta-da; a cheque for £106 is issued for collection at the local jobcentre.

I hope I manage to instil in you a good work ethic. Since your birth I've continued to do some kind of work; café work, writing, media work, speaking at events, support work, advocacy. When I've been unable to find employment, or been unable to work an average 9-5, I've created my own work, and I've done so in a way I can still spend time with you. I want you to have nice things, but I want you to understand that ultimately, you come first, and when it comes to working, I will always find a way to work around my commitment to you. If I wanted a lifestyle that revolved solely around my career, I wouldn't have continued on with the pregnancy.

Steff burns me a couple of lines, and I pass him the tooter back. I start telling him about the bullshit at home, and the incident the other day with the computer.

"So," he screws his face up, confused, "what was her actual reason for no lettin' you use the computer?"

I shrug, "fuck knows, but aye, she was happy for ma brother to sit and play fuckin minecraft, or whatever it is he was playing,"
He shakes his head as he runs a line, pulls the tooter out and quickly inhales a breath of air, taking the heroin deeper into his lungs, "what a fuckin cow man," he croaks.

I nod. I don't particularly like hearing other people speak about my mum that way, but he's not wrong. I'm so angry. And who the fuck can I actually speak to about it that will help?

There was only one person that ever helped with stuff like this, my dad.

If I even try to explain half of the shit, I'll sound like a fucking looney, which everyone thinks I am anyway because that's how I've been painted out to be. Mentally unstable, a liar. But I'm not.

But I am, apparently.

My phone beeps, a text from mum, my heart sinks – the normal reaction – what now?
I hope it's not an angry text, letting me know that she knows what I'm doing.

CHAPTER 6

Well, that didn't last long, did it? I knew it wouldn't. I'm actually surprised I was allowed to stay in the "family" home as long as I did.

My mum didn't kick me out. I left, because I knew it was coming.

I couldn't stay there any longer. It's like they expected me to get over dads' death within a day of the funeral. I've been told I don't really have the right to grieve, if anyone should be grieving, it's my brother – because he wasn't out running the streets taking smack.

I don't understand why we can't both grieve equally.

So, I stopped grieving.
I started taking gear again to stop the feelings. They kept telling me not to wallow in self-pity, or be dramatic, or use it as an excuse to relapse.
I'm not using his death as an excuse to relapse.
The excuse is – I've been told I shouldn't be grieving. And it's my family telling me this, so they must be right. But I just can't stop the feelings, the only thing that stops the feelings is getting high.

I just want my dad.

But now I'm using again, I know he wouldn't want me. I can't believe I've ended up back like this.

Steff and I are sitting in some guys flat. His name is Nicky, and he's in jail. The mortis lock on his front door wasn't secured, though, only the Yale – which is a piece of piss to bust open without actually breaking it. Even I can do it – I just shoulder-barge the door, and it opens. When it closes, the Yale lock clicks back into place. We can come, and go, without leaving behind any evidence that we've been coming and going.

We did originally get permission from Nicky to stay in the flat, with the intention of going to the council within a couple of days, but he ended up getting lifted, and jailed. And we've just been focusing on the gear, partially because we want to get smashed, but mainly because we overdone it and again, we need to stop the physical rattle.

Sitting right next to each other, on a tatty, 2-seater, leather couch that is an awful peach colour, we pass the tooter back and forth between us, taking 2 lines each at a time.

We've managed to get a teinth – 1.75g - to do us for the rest of the night, and a charge in the morning to get us up and out the door.

It's quite unusual for us to get this much, but we got lucky tonight; we went into the Tesco Express in Leith, expecting to maybe get about £20 worth of meat or cheese. When we got to the aisle, I spotted one of the cages that carries all the stock, just lying out in the middle of the floor.

Inside the cage was box after box of alcohol. Spirits.
We get £10 per litre bottle of spirits, that's standard. Doesn't matter how expensive it is.

£10/litre
£7.50/70cl
£2/bottle of wine.

Between me and him, we managed to get 9 bottles. Five in his backpack, and four in my handbag. Sold within 15 minutes.

The teinth cost £70, but it should last us a few burns.

I can feel my eyeballs beginning the process of rolling around in my head. It's the weirdest feeling. It's like if you pull a rubber band as far back as possible, without snapping it, and holding it in that position for 10 minutes. Eventually, you (and the rubber band), start shaking due to the tension.

That's what my eyeballs feel like.

And ping, I let go of the rubber band.
Fuck it. Eyes closed. Chin down. I'm fucking smashed.

Even though he's right next to me, his voice echoes, "comin' through to bed baby?".

I love it when he calls me baby, I don't know what it is, but it makes me feel, I dunno...

... Loved?

Bella, there's a reason that every time I address you, I call you Babygirl. Sweetheart. Darlin. My girl. My lassie. My Chicka. My Cheeky Monkey. My Smella-Bella, Bella-Capella.
My Beautiful-Scotland.

He helps me up off the couch, and holds my hand as we navigate through the dark hall, into the big, cold bedroom.
The walls are a darker shade of blue (not quite navy), the windows are tall, and old, letting all of the freezing cold air in through the gaps around the edges of the single panel glass. In the middle of the room is a basic divan bed, with a duvet and pillows, but now covers on them.

But neither myself or Steff really give a shit, because we're more interested in each other.

Suddenly, we can't feel the cold, regardless of our nakedness.

And regardless of my current situation, he makes me feel like the most gorgeous woman in the world. I'm not going to lie, physically, I don't feel much, he's never given me an orgasm. I've never had an orgasm.
But just the actual feeling of being there, with him, touching me, and showing me how much he loves me. It doesn't matter what he does when he's angry, because ultimately, I see the real him when it's just me and him, like we are now.

This is love.
This is what real love feels like.

Bella – don't ever confuse sex with love.

We are not just objects of sexual gratification.

2006
Around October/November.
14 years old.

I just don't want to fucking be here anymore.

I fucked up big time, and we all got caught.

Bella, we first got a computer with broadband when I was 12. I immediately became obsessed with going online and speaking on MSN messenger, like every one of my friends. And I soon discovered chatrooms.

Your Gran was so paranoid about paedophiles, online grooming, etc, but I can't ever remember her taking the time to actually sit and have a good look on the computer, if she did, she would've been mortified. And she was, when it all came out.

Her idea of online supervision was sitting on the couch watching television, whilst I sat at the back of her on the computer.

Talking to men in their thirties and forties.

Sex is love, remember?
I thought these men loved me.

I had lied and said I was 16, like every one of my friends did in chatrooms. But when things moved over to MSN messenger, which was private, I divulged the information, that really, I was only 13.

"Age is just a number,"
"Only a couple of years and it'll be legal for us to be together, what difference does it make if we're together now?"

I eventually ended up meeting 2 men – one was 40, the other was 36. And they fucking knew better, as adults.

But I knew better too, apparently, because I was soooooo intelligent. It was all my fault, if I hadn't initially told these guys I was 16, they wouldn't have added me, "fell in love" with me, and then continue to pursue me even after finding out my age.
No, none of that would've happened.
At 13 years old, I was manipulative, cunning, and just a wee slapper... apparently.

Nobody understood why I was the way I was. They thought they did, but they didn't.
And because they thought they did, they dealt with it the wrong way.

I wasn't given the love I so desperately sought from dangerous situations; I wasn't given understanding. I was berated, instead.

I'm sitting in a small room, just off reception, in the Young Persons Unit (**CAMHS**).

In front of me is my counsellor, and at the side of me is my mum. The meeting descended into Hell almost immediately, and now she's sitting and saying to my face that I'm a liar.

I've been seeing this counsellor for about 18 months, I think. All of our sessions have been just me and her, this is the first with my mum, ever. I really wanted this to be positive. And for her to just put the ego to the side, so we can work together and I can get in a place I don't feel like I have to seek love from other sources.

But within 5 minutes, she began branding me a liar, and attention seeker, to which the counsellor disagrees. All this does is make my mum irater.

Throughout the last 18 months, I've regularly told my counsellor, confidently, that I'm really struggling with a lot of things, mainly sleep. I can't sleep, I lie there awake, worrying.

I lie there, worrying, because I know when my mum and her arsehole husband go to bed, there's a very high chance I'm going to have to spend however long listening to them fuck as loudly and as hard as possible.

This isn't just occasionally waking up and hearing them go at it, while they clearly try to keep the noise down. No, it's outright shagging, and she's very vocal – and she's been made aware from myself, multiple times.

I remember before we were in Lochend, we were in Restalrig. I was around 9, maybe 10.
And I told her exactly what I could hear, and it was keeping me awake.
She asked me what time I go to sleep, and I told her I didn't know, probably around 1am.
She turned to her husband, in front of me, and said, "well, we'll have sex at 1am then".
I spent that night lying in bed, full of anxiety, unable to sleep because I *knew* I was going to hear it at some point.

It hurts. It hurts that she barely pays any attention to me, unless I'm in trouble, because she's working or whatever. But she'll go to bed every night with this dickhead and show him all the love in the world. And do it so loudly, that I get to hear every second. Like it's being rubbed in my face.

And now, here she is, her voice starting to raise, again branding me a compulsive liar. Claiming I haven't heard anything, and if I have, it's been once in a blue moon.

I'm crying now, and I tell her I just want her to keep it down, because it's really affecting me.

Her voice gets louder, **"So am I NOT allowed to have a sex life then?"**

The room suddenly goes silent, as me and the counsellor look at each other, both in shock.
It's becoming more and more obvious the counsellor is struggling to contain herself.

"Nobody said you couldn't have a sex life!" She responds, "your daughter is telling you that these noises make her extremely uncomfortable, she's just asking you to keep it down. Look, she's upset, don't you care that Azaria is crying?"

My mum raises her voice another decibel, "NO! I don't care!"

Again, the counsellor looks at me, speechless, and I begin physically crumbling in the seat
I can't stop crying.

"Di....di... did you really just say you don't care that your child is crying!?" the counsellor asks my mum.

"No! I don't!" My mum snaps back, "WHY SHOULD I CARE? It's her own fault she's crying! She's sitting there telling these lies, she has no reason to cry!"

I sob harder as I'm branded a liar again.

I've just had to walk away from the computer writing this, I'm really fucking angry.

I just want one whole week where I don't have to listen to my mum being ploughed. I don't want to hear moans, groans, and skin slapping. I just want to fucking sleep.

I just want a mum that's actually interested in me.

The session ends, and as my mum storms out in front of me, the counsellor stops me for a second.

She takes my hand, *"I believe you".*

To this day, your Gran maintains that counsellor was "just out to get her".

I know I'm in for Hell when we get home, and I'm right.

I go into my bedroom and listen as my mum sits there sobbing to that wanker, and then my Granny, telling them how I have made a total cunt of her by telling these outrageous lies, how she can't understand why I would tell such awful and malicious lies.

My bedroom door is knocked and I'm told to come out. It's Friday evening and Dad's here to take me and my brother for the weekend. I go through to the kitchen to leave through the front door, to be met by dickhead, and my Granny.

"See what you've done?" He starts.

Ah, here we go. The guy that also engages in the loud sex that I hear frequently, calling me a liar.

I'm told I should be grateful because I'm fed and clothed and not in care.

My Granny then shuffles over and leans into my face.
"You're nothing but a dirty prostitute".

CHAPTER 8

This morning started off with a bang.

Me and Steff woke up to Ritchies mum and auntie standing over us, screaming.

"WHO THE FUCK ARE YOUS? WHY THE FUCK ARE YOUS IN MY SONS HOUSE?"

Oh shit, time to go...

We got dressed as quickly as we could whilst they stood shouting and bawling. We told them that we did have Ritchies permission to be there when we turned up on the Friday, and he got lifted on Saturday. It's now Wednesday.

No, we haven't really got an excuse as to why we haven't gone to the council earlier, but if there ever was an excuse to present myself homeless, it was being thrown out of another addicts house by their mother.

Fuck sake man.

It's fucking freezing, and because she woke us up, it's not like we've had time to get a burn in us this morning! Fuck!

Not to worry. Up until 12pm, all of the stairs are accessible by pressing the service button, which is only for the postmen.
We jump into the communal stair next door to Nickys, and begin preparing the tinfoil. Steff bursts out laughing.

????????????????????

He puts his hand in his pocket, and pulls out an envelope.

"Look," he starts opening it, "mind Nicky said he was due £400 backdated money from the dole? Well, look what I clocked when we were walking out the door.

In his hand is a cheque for £410.

Ya fuckin beauty.

It's not like Nicky needs it – he's got it sound in jail, in a wee cell with a TV, medication and 3 meals a day. Plus, whatever money his mum hands in to him for tobacco and munchies.

We take it to one of those cheque cashing places, you don't need ID to prove it belongs to you, as long as you pay a fee to the place. We get about £390.

Still better than fuck all.

Life is good.

Things like this really keep me positive. Like a sign that things will get better.

No, no, no, no, no.
There was no sign.
Only crime.

CHAPTER 9

Woodchip ceilings.

I can't escape woodchip ceilings.

Here I am, again, lying on my back, questioning everything about my life, whilst staring at a fucking woodchip ceiling.

Most of the worst parts of my life have taken place under a woodchip ceiling.

Whether I'm in a drug den, gouching out. Or back in my mums' house.
It's always under a woodchip ceiling.

It's funny how you notice these things.

Right now, I'm in a council bed and breakfast with Steff.

And at this exact moment, I'm lying on the floor, looking up at the woodchip ceiling. Crying.

Steff comes out of the bathroom and starts making his way out of the room to leave.

As he walks past, he lifts his leg up.
He brings his foot back down at full velocity, onto my hand, and he twists his heel into my fingers.

Crunch.

But the pain doesn't really register, because it's absolutely NOTHING compared to the pain running around inside of my head right now.

I just want to run away and never see another woodchip ceiling in my life.

CHAPTER 10

This bed and breakfast really isn't that bad. But I think it's because the guy that runs it is very obviously a bit dodgy – the entire building smells like weed, and he's made it clear he doesn't give a shit if we smoke, too. As long as we run over the road to score a £20 bit of grass when he can't be arsed, we're sound.

His mum comes in every Wednesday to do the cleaning. She's a nice lady, often brings us actual cooked food. Woman is in her 60s and cleans every corner of every room in this old Victorian house, whilst her son – the B&B manager – sits on his arse "managing" his cannabis habit.

It's early in the morning, and I'm woken by male voices shouting out in the hallway, above us. We're on the first floor, and the top floor is above us.

It's Stevie, the manager, I can make his voice out. I can hear another guy, but fuck knows what he's saying, I think he might be pished or something.

I sit up.

"Shh," Steff holds his finger out, "listen".

We sit silently, in the bed, next to the room door, listening to the aggression unfolding over our heads.

"GOAN," Stevies voice suddenly becomes clear as he steps out of a room on the floor above us into the hall, "GOAN! FUCK OFF! DIRTY OLD ALKY BASTARD!"

Me and Steff look at each other, and I point up to the ceiling, using sign language to ask if it's the poor old alcoholic above us he's shouting at. Steff nods.

The guy can barely string a sentence together, but I don't think he's had a drink. I think that's just how he is, because of the alcohol, it's like he's brain damaged.

It's a fucking shame.

But Stevie unleashes a barrage of insults on the poor man, as he simultaneously screams at him to get the fuck out of the B&B.

"Fuckin DIRTY OLD PISHY ARSED ALKY CUNT,"

Bella, I remember every word.

I can hear them getting closer as they move down the stairs, and suddenly, they're outside of our room door. I'm shaking hard; I don't like violence. I'm really scared. This is fucked up.

Thud. Thudthudthudthudthudthudthudthud.

And laughing.

"Ha!" Stevie erupts, "stupid old cunt "fell" down the stairs".

The sounds of this man lying at the bottom of the staircase, confused, in pain, and groaning, will never, ever leave my head.

Steff jumps up and swings the room door open. Stevie is now standing in the middle of the stairs, with the biggest smile on his face.

"You alright mate? What's happenin?" Steff questions.

"Awch, this smelly auld bastard mate... Look!! Fuckin LOOK! He's pissed all over the floor!"

He explodes again, "AM GONNAE HAVE TO FUCKIN CLEAN THAT!! FUCKIN DIRTY SMELLY CUNT MAN! GET FUCKIN OOT!"

I've got my fingers in my ear but I can hear every word.

Oh my god, I just want to get out of here.

CHAPTER 11

The bed and breakfast is in Tollcross, so basically the city centre.

Do you know how fucking convenient that is for a shoplifter?

When normal people move into a new area, they go looking for the best amenities, schools, doctors' practices...

When a shoplifter moves into a new area, they go hunting for the best shops, the easiest shops to steal from, the ones that have the better and more expensive stock.

This is the posher area of town, ain't no B&M bargain stores selling cheap, useless shite here. Nope.

Waitrose. I'm stealing from Waitrose.
Moving up in the world.

Well, I intend on stealing from Waitrose, like I did yesterday. It was an absolute canter, couldn't believe how absurdly easy it was to chore from.

So, before we left, I put some makeup on, some decent looking, clean clothes, and grabbed my biggest, nicest handbag.

Plan is the same as yesterday; Steff goes in initially, looking rough as fuck, to distract the security guard. And whilst he's doing that, I'll head in, go straight to the alcohol aisle, grab 2 or 3 bottles of spirits, and casually walk out as if I've forgotten my purse at home.

It's a solid plan, worked a charm yesterday.

No two days are ever the same, hen.

As we approach Waitrose, Steff speeds up and I slow down, and I watch as he strolls into Waitrose looking suspicious as fuck. I slow down again to make sure there's enough time for the security guard to spot him before I go in.

Walking in the doors, I can't see him or a security guard anywhere. Perfect - he's obviously taking the silly cunt on a run-around around the shop, avoiding the end aisle at all costs.

I take the opportunity and make my way to the alcohol aisle. I'm so confident, that for once I'm actually not dying inside. And the confidence shows in my actions, as I hold my head up high walking into the aisle, trying my hardest not to look suspicious.

As soon as the last customer leaves the aisle, and before the next customer arrives in the aisle, I pick up 2 bottles of triple distilled vodka and quietly place them into my bag. I shuffle it about very gently once they're in, so they settle properly, and don't clank together when I'm walking out. As soon as I finish shuffling, a customer appears, and I take that as my queue to exit the shop.

Still as confident as ever, I make my way back to the entrance of the shop, to leave.

As I turn the corner of the last aisle. Fuck.

Security guard, right at the fucking door.

I start panicking internally, but still trying to remain calm on the outside.

Oh fuck I want to cry.

I can actually feel the walls closing in on me, I've made a huge mistake.

HUGE mistake man.

Fuckfuckfuck, what a FUCKING IDIOT!

And then I snap back to reality – I've no choice but to deal with this.
Not only that, but I imagine it's not waiting for me. It's obviously for Steff! He's the one that came in looking as shifty as they come, he probably just wants to make sure Steff definitely doesn't have anything in his bag before he leaves the shop.

Plus, if he was on to me, I know for a fact Steff would've made a point of finding me, walking past, and whispering to abort mission.

Turns out, Bella, that when I walked in and didn't see either of them, that was because Steff didn't even get to take the security guard a wild goose-chase around the shop, because within 30 seconds of walking in, he bumped into security – who quickly escorted him off the premises through a fire exit at the back of the shop, informing him he had watched our whole scheme on CCTV yesterday, after we left.

Fingers are digging deep into my upper-arm. Really fucking deep. Wait, that's more than just a hard grip – this security guard is twisting my fucking arm!!!

I scream with the pain of my skin being twisted.
And because I scream, he starts shouting that I'm resisting, and literally lifts me off the ground by my upper arm.
He begins dragging me to where the office is – upstairs, but I'm struggling to keep up because I'm so focused on the pain in my arm. I'm stuttering as I plead with him to loosen his grip.

As we reach the first step, he suddenly increases his walking speed and the edge of my foot bumps into the first step, sending me plummeting to the ground. But of course, this honey-monster has got a grip of my arm, so I don't really hit the ground fully – I just hang there like a doll.

And I hang there, desperately kicking my feet trying to get them back flat on the ground, as he drags me up the stairs, dipping his arm slightly with every couple of steps to make sure I hit them.

This is a bit fucking dramatic over a few bottles of vodka, mate.

This is a full-blown assault.

I swear this cunt has transported us, and he's actually dragging me step-by-step up the Eiffel Tower, because these steps just don't seem to fucking end. It's like he's moving super-fast, but my perception is super slow. He's steaming up the steps so fast that I don't have time to actually register when they stop, and as we reach the last step and he's dragging me along a hall, still twisting my arm, it takes a few seconds for me to realise I can actually put both feet on the ground.

Even if it's only for a millisecond, before he rips me along again, pulling me off my feet.

The door to an office is swung open, and he physically swings me back to gain momentum, and then forward into the office. Right into a desk chair.

Holy fucking shit.

This ain't fucking normal, there's no justification for this assault. I mean, I get being angry, but this is beyond angry.

Bella, he was angrier than Steff the New Years he wanted to kill me. I've never seen fury like this.

What's wrong, son?
What's up with this pure, burning hatred for shoplifters?
Did your mother have an affair with a shoplifter?
Were you brought up in some dusty, African village, your family the local tinkers, that stole left, right and centre. You seen the abuse they were subjected to trying to survive, and you swore never to be one of them.
Did you try and stop a female shoplifter, and she bent you over and sodomised you?

I really don't understand this guys anger. There's about a minute of silence, as I sit in the chair, reeling from the assault, as all 6'4" of this man stands directly over me, with his arms folded, face screwed up like a furious pitbull. He doesn't blink.

Is this the terminator?

The office door swings open again, and in walks a manager. He looks pretty pissed off, but an acceptable level of pissed off. He's just looking at me shaking his head. He informs me he's phoned the police.

That's a fucking relief, to be honest. It really is.

As soon as the manager asks the security to explain what happened from start to finish, the guys demeanour changes from this enraged animal, to an excited toddler that's just done their first shit in the potty.

He is genuinely to formulate a complete sentence, as he stumbles over his words, giddy with joy.

I am honestly not exaggerating hen, this is honestly what happened. And I'm sitting laughing right now, he was a fucking dick.

I refuse to speak to either of these men, which almost sends the security guard into cardiac arrest with anger.

I will only speak to the police.

Security scoffs that he hates people like me.

It's people like me keeping you in a fucking job pal.

A female manager walks into the office, and that doesn't ease me anxiety. Why should it? She works for the shop too, she's on "their" side. She's gonna be just as much of a cunt as tweedledee and tweedledum standing in front of me with their fingers up their arses.

She sits in a chair infront of me, an introduces herself as the head manager. She seems really nice, I'm suspicious, but starting to feel less anxious.
She begins to explain that per Waitrose policy, she has to fill in this form for every shoplifter. Just all my basic details.

Word of advice – if you ever get caught shoplifting (and I hope to god you don't ever feel the need to steal), do not fall for this. DO NOT GIVE THEM YOUR NAME.
Because not only will the police arrest and charge you for the offence, the shop will take your details and start civil proceedings against you to try and recover some of the money they lost due to your five-finger discount. Plus money for the hassle of dealing with you.

After taking my details, she puts the form down, and leans forward, "can I just ask... Why were you in shoplifting today and yesterday?"

Shit, that's the trigger. It's like when you're having a shitty time, and someone asks if you're okay – you immediately break down.

I tell her the truth. That I was in shoplifting to support my heroin habit, because if I didn't, I knew Steff would smash me.

Her eyebrows lower in sympathy, and a staff member pops her head in the office door and lets us know the police are downstairs.

Oh my fucking God, did the security guard REALLY just high-five the manager? REALLY?

My feelings of upset dwindle as I can't control my laughter, and now the police are literally coming upstairs now, there's sweet fuck all security can do to hurt me.

Ha ha.

He spins around and I swear I think he's going to bolt across the room and punch me clean through the fucking wall.

"I don't know why you're laughing," he points in my face, "you're going to pay"

I'm smiling back, because I know any second the police will be in the door, "I won't pay anything mate".

He screws his face up, like he doesn't get what I mean.

"This is literally my first charge, ever. Like, ever. I can promise you now, I'll be released either on caution, or police bail from the station, I'll get a fiscal fine, that'll come directly out my benefits a fiver a week,"

He still doesn't seem to understand.

"YOU'RE the taxpayer, mate," I spell it out, "You pay my benefits. So no, you're the one that needs to pay".

And it's at that moment, the police walk in, and the female officer sits down beside me.

I don't know what's been said, but she asks if I'm okay. I tell her I'm far from okay.

"Are you injured?" She gently asks me.

Oh no, tears are starting again. I'm sniffling.

"My knee is bruised a bit, my arms really sore but there's no mark, I don't think," I tell her.

She asks to see, and there's a clear red mark. But it won't bruise.

Information is swapped, and they don't put cuffs on me – my wrists are genuinely far too small for handcuffs.

The put me into the back of the car, and as the male officer starts the engine, he looks back to me, "don't worry pal, we're just taking you up to St.Leonards because we have to – you'll be out in a couple of hours".

He then turns to the female officer, and lets out a stifled laugh, "he was a bit excited, wint he?"

I was released with a caution.

AZARIA FAVER

CHAPTER12

Every day is the same.

Every. Fucking. Day. Is. The. Fucking. Same.

I'm not even joking, there is no exaggeration here.

I wake up, and don't immediately reach for coffee, or go for a shower. I get dressed, and go out for a shoplift. If I don't Steff goes alone, but makes sure I suffer for it. He'll come back with a bag, and sit there smoking it in front of me whilst I sit there visibly withdrawing. And between lines, he'll make remarks, like "feeling shit, aye?", "Rattling?"

He fucking knows I am.

So, we go out, sell whatever we get at a corner shop or pub, go score, come back, have a charge, go right back out for a shoplift. Sell the stuff. Score. Come back. Have a charge. And then we go straight back out for a shoplift. Sell the stuff. Score Come back. Have a charge and then we go straight back out for a shoplift. Sell the stuff. Score. Come back. Have a charge. And then we go straight back out. Sell the stuff. Score Come back. Have a charge and then we go straight back out for a shoplift. Sell the stuff. Score. Come back. Have a charge. And then we go straight back out. Sell the stuff. Score Come back. Have a charge and then we go straight back out for a shoplift. Sell the stuff. Score. Come back. Have a charge. And then we go straight back out. Sell the stuff. Score Come back. Have a charge and then we go straight back out for a shoplift. Sell the stuff. Score. Come back. Have a charge. And then we go straight back out. Sell the stuff. Score Come back. Have a charge and then we go straight back out for a shoplift. Sell the stuff. Score. Come back. Have a charge. And then we go straight back out. Sell the stuff. Score Come back. Have a charge and then we go straight back out for a shoplift.

I can't believe this is actually my fucking life.

CHAPTER 13

It's been a breeze of a day.

Along Dalry, there's a big Co-op, it used to be a Summerfield. They only put security tags on the bottles of alcohol sitting at the front, to give the illusion that all of their stock is bugged. But the bottles at the back of the shelves aren't tagged.

To add to that, they have two entrances/exits, and only one of them actually have the security tag scanners. Even if you can only get to the bugged bottles, you can still walk out without setting off the alarms.

Worst case scenario – we have to use tinfoil to wrap around the tags, it blocks the door scanner picking up the signal as you pass through.

Between me and Steff, we got 9 bottles of spirits. NINE!

£90!

We've got enough for a teinth, tobacco, and food.

As Steff exits a phone box, after speaking to our dealer, he tells me I have to run up to the guys house for it, because he can't be bothered with him. No problem.

The guy is called Robbie, and he's only 5 minutes away. I've only met him a handful of times when he's came out to meet us, I've never been up to his house. He seems like an okay guy – looks like a proper rough junkie, but he seems sound.

We cross over a dual carriageway, and Steff dives into a bus stop whilst I walk over to the row of flats that stand 5 floors high. I press the buzzer, Robbie answers, and I go into the stair. He's on the top floor.

Chapping his letterbox to let him know I'm there, there's silence for a minute or so, and I can see light coming and going behind his peephole, suggesting to me that he's having a spy to make sure it is me.

Suddenly, the door swings open. But Robbie isn't there, and I stand looking straight ahead into the hall, confused.

"Get doon!" I hear his voice snap at me, from the floor.

I look down and he's lying on his front, propped up on his elbows, looking up at me. I'm totally taken aback, what the fuck does he mean get down!?
Why!?

Again, he hisses, "Azaria! Get fuckin doon!"

For some reason, I actually get down on the ground, and army crawl my way into the flat. He swings the door closed, reaches up to lock it, and tells me to stay low, as he then drags himself past me to lead the way into the living room. I stay as low as I can and shuffle along the hall behind him, all I can see is the bottom of his socks. They're black, but they look like they were originally white.

We get into the living room, and he closes the door, shuffles over to a space on the floor in front of the TV, where he has a tray with his smack set up on it. You know, the usual dealer shit – gear, bags, scales, a scoop, scissors.

He waves his hand, motioning for me to crawl over to where he is, so he can show me my teinth on the scales, assuring me it isn't short.

He bites the long tail off the plastic baggie and flings the teinth to me, "they've been watching me for the last 2 days".

"Who?" I ask.

"Who do you think!?" He scoffs, as if I should know, "the fuckin polis!"

My heart sinks, as I realise this stupid cunt has allowed me to come up to his house, whilst he's convinced the police are watching him.

That's right, mate, you just allow me to get caught up in whatever drug raid is due to happen.

He points out of the window, over to clear sky, "they've been watching me from there, with binoculars!"

And it suddenly dawns on me that, being on the top floor, nobody could watch through the windows anyway.

I humour his obvious psychotic theory, and tell him to stay safe, as I spin around on my front and start army crawling my way back out of the living room, down the hall, to the front door.

What the actual fuck am I doing.
What is wrong with me man.

"Oh!" Robbie chirps behind me as we reach the front door, "let me get that for you hen".

He drags himself forward past me with his elbows, and reaches up to unlock the door.

To actually open the door so I can get out, is like the Krypton factor.
Like a game of twister, it takes a couple of minutes for both of us to untangle our legs as he struggles to pull the door open from the ground, and I try to move over to the side to give the door room to open.

Fingers locked in front of me, I move each elbow forward one at a time, and move past the threshold of the flat, out into the communal stair.

"Catch you later hen!" He smiles, as he leans back and swings the door shut again.

As soon as it's closed, I jump back up onto both feet and storm down the stairs.

Laughter explodes from me as I exit the stair and make eye contact with Steff.

He smiles, looking confused at the same time, "What is it?"

I take a deep breath to try and control my laughter, *"Ken what? I don't even fucking know,"*.

CHAPTER 14

Six hours. Six fucking hours.

SIX FUCKING HOURS!

It's taken us SIX FUCKING HOURS to get our FIRST shoplift today.

Normally it takes us an hour at the very max. On the odd occasion it's taken a couple of hours.

Of course, it's all my fault, according to Steff. He tried to get a bag on tick earlier on, the guy said no, and when he was coming out of the phone box, he slammed the door of it into the side of my face unexpectedly. I spent the remaining 3 hours walking about feeling like I couldn't breathe, trying to hold the tears in because I knew if I started crying, he would smash me. I don't understand why he's so angry and being so nasty, I'm rattling just as much as him.

We eventually got into the big Scotmid at 7pm, when the security guard went on his break. We sat opposite the shop, hiding behind a phone box, waiting for him to disappear into the back of the shop. As soon as he did, we crossed the road and went in.

Between us, we got about £45 of stuff. It was actually a lot more but we were so, so fucking ill we sold it for the first price we were offered. Fuck it, we NEED a burn.

It's just before 9pm by the time we get back to the bed and breakfast. As soon as we both set foot inside the bedroom, we don't even take our shoes off – we sit down on the shitty leather couch that sits at the end of our bed, and Steff pulls out the foil from underneath him, rips off a sheet, and starts burning the gear in nice, neat lines down the foil.

We're sitting on the green, leather couch that sits at the end of the double bed. Well, I'm sitting at the end, squished into the arm, because Steff is lying outstretched. I feel like he's purposely digging his feet into me, like a punishment for him being in a shitty mood.

He takes one line and then two. And then three. And four. And five.

"Fuck sake, Steff," I don't even know why I'm opening my mouth here, "I thought we went two-for-two?"

The ball joint in my hip feels like it's been rattled into with a 14lb hammer as he uses all the energy the smack has obviously given him to boot me in the side with his heel, as hard as he feels is necessary.

I'm not crying.
I'm not fucking doing it.

He takes another couple of lines, and then passes the tooter over to me so he can burn my lines for me.

I'm just grateful he's sharing it. He's made it clear he doesn't need to, so he obviously does care that I'm rattling or he wouldn't be sharing it at all.

CHAPTER 15

Me: Mum im srry,cnt do this nymore.i knw u dnt want me home but I dnt know what else to do

Mum: R u ok

Me: No

She phones me, my voice is really shaky. It's October, so it's been a few months since I left and obviously things weren't good then. I just don't know what else to do. I can't do it anymore. I can't do this anymore, or I'm going to kill myself. Seriously, if I stay another day, I will kill myself. That is a promise. I can't deal with this. It's too much, I never thought things would be this bad again, especially after my dad died.

I can't stop crying.

Steff told me to go, because I refused to go out shoplifting. He threw my huge suitcase at me, and then began throwing my belongings around the room. Shouting at me to leave and go fuck whoever I want to fuck. The usual shit. It was like a light switch.

So, I'm leaving.

I'm standing at the window, watching for my mums car with my suitcase ready. Everything ready.

Oh, fuck. Here he is.

Well, he made it clear he doesn't want me here.

My heart still batters against my chest as I follow him with my eyes, walking up the path, and pressing the bell for entry. The front door opens to let him in, and within a minute the bedroom door is opening.

He rushes into the bedroom, with tears in his eyes.

"Baby," He starts, "Please."
"No, Steff," I reply bluntly.

I'm not staying.

He begins to bubble, and for what feels like the first time ever, I genuinely don't have any guilt, or sadness for him. None. He done this.

"Steff," I speak a bit louder, "I'm going, my mums on her way."
He holds out our shared mobile phone, "Please, baby, please, just phone her and tell her it's okay."

I screw my face up and tell him there's no way I'm just telling my mum to go home. As I do so, he's trying to force the phone into my hands, to make the call.

When he realises that I'm just not going to call her, he raises it above his head and smashes it on the cord carpet. His mouth is doing that thing where the corners turn downwards, his teeth are clenched, but his lips are open slightly, and there's bubbles forming along his teeth as he puts on his most dramatic display yet.

And thank fuck, here's mum.

Well, I suppose this cunt isn't going to help me down the stairs with my suitcase, is he?

I barely lift the suitcase a few inches off the floor, and struggle down the stairs with it. As I walk out of the building, I refuse to look up at the window – I can feel his eyes burning into me.

I put my stuff in the boot of the car, and jump into the passenger seat.

"Are you okay, hen?" Mum asks, sympathetically.
I smile gently and nod.

She then looks up at the bedroom window, towards Steff.
"Awww," as if she is looking at a puppy in a window, "Look at him. What a shame."

And suddenly I regret calling her.

CHAPTER 16

I've been back "home" for a month. I already feel like I've overstayed my welcome, although I will say my mum and Billy aren't being anywhere near as bad as they were just after Dad died. Probably because he blatantly ignores me, and my brother, at all opportunities.

Again, I've been really trying hard for a job, and I think they can actually see that, because they haven't nipped away at my head about job hunting like they have done before.

Things between me and my mum are... Okay, I suppose. As long as I do and act exactly as she expects, no going off track, things will be good. She's been taking me to get my hair, tan, and nails done at her friends' salon. It's not really my thing, to be honest, I do like it but it's just not... me? I don't think it's me. But, if I were to walk about how I would normally choose to walk about, I'll be reminded it's not the right choice.
I suppose my mum just wants things to look perfect, I don't blame her.

Bella, I couldn't give a shit if things look perfect.

I'm sitting upstairs using an older laptop she had given me, sitting on MSN messenger. I've sent out all of the CVs I can send, I've applied for all jobs that are appropriate, so I don't have much else to do.
It's times like these I wish I could go and get fucked, like out of my nut away with it. But things are going well here, and it's not like I could if I wanted to – I don't have the money. I've been home all month, and still haven't spoken to Steff. I'm not interested.

Walking into the kitchen, I feel the harsh change in atmosphere as my mum, and auntie, fall completely silent. I assume they were talking about something completely private, so it doesn't faze me – I just keep walking in, bend down to get a can of juice from the bottom shelf, and stand back up.

As soon as I am back upright, and make eye contact with my mum, she screws her face up and snaps, "What have you taken, Azaria?"

I freeze. I did not expect a question like that, at all. I genuinely have no fucking idea what she's on about. I've been home all week; I've been in my room all night. I'm wracking my mind trying to think of a single explanation as to why she would think I'm on something right now.
Maybe I look tired? I don't fucking know!
Seriously, I don't!!!

So, I stand there, chin lowered in shock, and I try to formulate a response back, "Wha...What are you on about? I've been upstairs all night..." I begin my feeble attempt at defending myself.

She widens her eyes and straightens her back, like a fucking python, "DON'T lie to me. Look at the state of you!"

I'm physically shaking now because I genuinely, really don't understand what is making her think I've taken something.

I wish I had fucking taken something!

The tears in my eyes are being held back by some invisible force, the same force pushing the lump up my throat, "Mum..." I'm almost bubbling, "What do you mean look at the state of me!? I've been home all fucking night!"

She raises her voice again, as my auntie sits next to her with her arms folded, lips pursed, giving me dirty looks, "What did I just say? DON'T argue with me Azaria, do you think I'm stupid?"

"Well, WHAT am I doing that makes me apparently look like am out ma nut!?"

"Don't raise your voice at me!"

I ask her again, whilst fighting back the tears.

49

"Just get out!" And she motions for me to leave the kitchen.

I don't understand why she couldn't tell me what her reason was.

Was there even a fucking reason, man?

I just don't get it; I don't get it.

I leave the kitchen, and my feet pound each step back upstairs as I make my way back into the bedroom, where the party's at, apparently.

I'm looking in the mirror, and carefully inspecting every part of my face, my body, my body language, everything. I'm searching for the singular reason that is currently making me look like I'm under the influence of... something?

I don't even know what I'm meant to be high on!

Fuck this shit.
I'm phoning Steff.

CHAPTER 17

Well, I came back. I fucking came back.

Because if I'm getting accused of it anyway, I might as well go out and take something. I may as well enjoy myself if I'm gonna get blamed for it regardless. Fuck it.

Of course, I phoned Steff.
And of course, he immediately answered, and told me to go see him. He's finally been given a flat in Tollcross, so just around the corner from the B&B we were in.

Typical, I leave him and 6 weeks later he's offered a permanent flat.

It's okay, nothing to write home about. The housing officer took a bit of pity on him and left all of the previous tenants furniture. Normally they take everything out, rip the carpets up, I think they have to for health & safety reasons. But she seen he had nothing, so left everything.

I think the previous tenant was a pensioner, probably a single guy. The couch is spotless, but looks like something from the 1940s. On the other side of the living room is a basic double futon, in a pale red colour. Nothing is matching. But who gives a shit?

The first time seeing Steff after such a dramatic ending is always nerve wracking. I always spend the time travelling to meet him, regretting the meeting in advance. But I don't feel like I have any other option. I really don't.

It's either stay at home and be constantly fucking picked at and degraded in the most passive-aggressive ways, or come to Steff and deal with him and all of his problems.

At least with Steff, I can have a charge. It's the only positive thing in my life.

Seriously, heroin is the only positive, I know that sounds pure bizarre. It sounds ridiculous, nobody understands. It just makes me feel... better.

Anyway, it's been two weeks now, since I left "home" again. I don't know why I even call it home, it's not a home.

I don't have a home and I never fucking did, not a normal one.

Fuck this.

We're back to the shoplifting on a daily basis to support our habit. Smoking about a half-teinth a day between us, so like £40.
And shoplifting around here is a fucking breeze, because it's the city centre, there's so many places to steal from. And so many places to sell it.

I didn't want to be back here, but I didn't want to be stuck in a house where people just don't understand me, and put me down for what they don't understand. People who consistently put barriers in front of me, and then bitch about me when I can't cross them.

Fuck, it's been a hard day. It took us a good hour to get our first chore, and then took us until 8pm to finally get another chore when the security guard in Sainsburys went on his break. Got in, straight to the second aisle, and filled out bags with big jars of coffee. It was a fucking relief to be able to walk into a shop and not be spotted straight away.

We scored, and now we're sitting smoking our gear. I feel so relaxed, after a full day of walking about in awful Scottish weather, all I've wanted is to sit down, and have a burn.

CHAPTER 18
PART 1

My head feels heavy, it's a weird feeling. It's still really early, probably around 7am, and my throat is so dry – I genuinely cannot swallow.

God knows why I feel so crappy, I shouldn't be rattling. We've been going out for our first shoplift of the day at like 9am, normally get a tenner bag by 10am. So, I've still got a few hours before I start feeling really bad.

Steff is still sleeping. We decided to pull the futon out in the living room last night, and fell asleep watching TV. It's right next to the kitchen door, so I carefully step over him as I go to get a drink.

I open the fridge, and all that's there to drink is a mouthful of milk. I know I shouldn't drink it, because Steff loves his milk, especially in the morning, but I really need something cold to soothe my throat.

It's no big deal, we've got £2 there. I'll nip down to the shop when he wakes up so he's got milk for a drink.

As soon as I lie back down on the futon, he's awake. And he does not seem like he is in a good mood.

My heart sinks, I know what kind of day it's going to be.

My heart sinks further as I remember I've drank the last of the milk.

My heart keeps sinking as he begins walking through to the kitchen, to get a drink of milk.

Like he does every morning.

Fuck sake Azaria, why are you so stupid?
You KNOW he drinks milk every morning, without fail.
I should've drunk fucking water.

My hearts pounding.

"WHERE'S THE FUCKING MILK?"

Oh no.

I can't answer, because he bounces the hard bottom of the milk jug off my nose. I instinctively put my hands over my face, and before I open my eyes, I feel a pressure on top of me.

He's straddling me, on the futon, and puts his hands around my neck.

"If you EVER drink the last of the milk again..." he snarls through gritted teeth, "...I'll cut your fucking throat!"

All I can do is croak the word okay through tears.
He lets go, gets up, and sits over on the other couch, to begin smashing me with a tirade of verbal bullshit.
And, as he smashes and smashes and smashes away at my being with the language-focused assault, I unlock our mobile phone, and open up the browser.

Oh shit, Facebook!
I thought we ran out of data, but I must have a wee bit left.

As he slows down on the name-calling, he sits back.
Ah, it's one of these days, I see.

He often does this thing where he'll wake up in the morning, and just not get ready to go out. It almost always results in me begging him to go for a shoplift, and he revels in it. I can genuinely see it in his face, as he sits there with a smug smile, watching me fall deeper into withdrawal.
If I don't start begging, he kicks off fully. He'll suddenly jump off the couch, and start throwing things about, or slap me, and tell me it's just because he felt like it.

Fuck this.

I have no idea how much data is left, but I know it won't be much, so I quickly share a post to my newsfeed, asking for help, that I've just been strangled over milk, I need to get out of here, and put the phone back down.
Within five minutes, the phone rings, and it's my mum.
Fuck, I can't answer, I'm too scared, he'll go mental.

"What's she phoning for?" Steff questions.

Oh my god, I feel sick now.

I tell him I don't know, and go back to just sitting on the couch.
Fuck this, I'm not begging, and I'm not cowering when he starts going mental. I absolutely refuse to give him the reaction he wants.

After 15 minutes, he's starting to get restless on the couch, and I'm sitting here waiting. Just fucking waiting on the eruption. Any minute now...

There's a chap at the door. I rush up to get it.

And he fucking knows.

He stands up behind me, and tears have miraculously appeared in his eyes, "Baby..."

"I'm going, Steff..." I begin, as I start flinging belongings into a handbag on my way to the door.

He starts bubbling, "...bu-bu-but, why?"

"You literally just strangled me and threatened to cut my throat over MILK!"

He looks perplexed, "What? I didn't do that!"

"OH MY GOD!" I shout, and shake my head.

Nah, no fucking way. No fucking way is this man actually standing there telling me NONE of what happened, actually happened.
Is he actually fucking serious!?!?

I unlock the front door, and swing it open, expecting to see my mum.

Holy fuck, it's Uncle Gio, and suddenly I regret calling for help.

Shitshitshitshitshitshitshitshit.

He takes one step over the threshold of the flat, puts his hands on both of my shoulders, and leans in until his nose is only about a centimetre away from mine.
Hermly tells me to ignore whatever happens in the living room, to go get my stuff so we can leave.

CHAPTER 18
PART 2

Steffs screams echo throughout the house, I've never heard him like this. The terror in his squeals is making my entire body shake.

I've managed to get pretty much everything I need without going into the living room, avoiding the ruckus that is getting louder and more violent by the second.

I'm halfway out of the door with Granny Milkshake when, shit, my medication!
I've been on anti-depressants for months now, and I'll withdraw if I don't take them. But they're in the kitchen, and I need to walk through the living room to get there.

Shit.
But I really need them, like really need them.

So, I tell my Granny, who drills it into me to get my meds as quickly as possible so we can get the fuck out of here.

I do as I'm told, and without actually looking or focusing on anything going on, I run through the living room to the kitchen, and put my pills in my bag.
As I turn to go back out, I see 2 big kitchen knives. I realise this is the one chance I've got to get rid of the knives, before Steff gets a hold of them. He's obsessed with knives and stabbing people, I know if he gets a chance to get into this kitchen for the knives, then he will.

I hide them both on top of the boiler, and continue making my way back to Granny, who is still in the hall waiting on me.

Rushing through the living room, I make the biggest mistake I could make – I actually *look* at what's going on.

FUCK!

Initially, all I can see is my uncles back, and there doesn't seem to be much movement – that's what made me look.

I then decide to look further, and run over to the corner of the room.

FUCK!!!

Steffs face looks like that of a drowning victim; bright red, bloated, with his swollen tongue poking out of his purple lips.
My uncle is using the cord from my straighteners to strangle him. As in – he is properly attempting to murder Steff!

I don't know what the fuck to do, but I know enough to know NOT to kick off at my uncle, or I'll make it worse for myself, and then everyone else.

"UNCLE GIO!" I shout, "HE'S NEARLY DEED! LET'S GO!"

I pull at his shoulder, and he twists his head around to make eye contact with me.
He gives me the weirdest look; I don't think I'm ever gonna forget it. I dunno how to describe it, but he looks like he's just snapped out of a trance, and he immediately regrets his prior choices.

We both begin making our way out of the flat, and when we get to the hall, we both realise that Granny isn't there.

"Where's yer granny!?" Uncle Gio snaps.

The answer is literally on the tip of my tongue, but I'm unable to verbalise the fact that I don't know where she is – when I turn to answer him, I see Steff steaming towards us at full speed with a big kitchen knife in each hand.

Uncle Gio pushes me out of the front door, swings it shut and stands holding it, as Steff – on the other side of the door – is going ballistic trying to pull the door open.
Suddenly, a knife pokes my uncle in the hip, and we both look

down to see Steff ramming the knives through the letterbox, trying to stab my uncle.

He's starting to struggle holding the door closed, "I canny hold this door much longer, Azaria!" His arms are shaking, "Am gonnae let go of the handle, as soon as I do, YOU FUCKIN RUN!"

He lets go of the handle, and we both start running. He stays behind me, so if Steff does catch up, I'll get away.

I need to find Granny. I NEED TO FIND GRANNY.

My 74-year-old granny is fucking missing and Steff is on the loose with 2 kitchen knives!!!
FUCK!

I start throwing myself down multiple stairs at a time – we're coming down from the 5th floor. The whole way I'm throwing myself down these steps, all I can think is "granny, granny, granny... where the fucks my granny!?"

My biggest fear is that he stabs my uncle, and catches my granny too.

I get to the bottom of the stairs, and she's still nowhere. Oh no. Oh no.

Running outside, relief slaps me in the face as I hear her shouting for me, telling me to hurry up and get in her car.

Behind me, Uncle Gio comes running out, and we pile into the car with only 2 seconds to spare – Steff is at the back of us, still yielding 2 knives, and oh boy, is he pissed the fuck off.

He makes eye contact with me, and pokes the tip of his finger off the window as he snarls at me, "YOU...I'M GOING TO FUCKING KILL YOU"

He starts booting the car window, determined to get into me.

Uncle Gio starts loudly laughing at him, and pointing back, "Ahaha, look at you, fuckin' DAFTY,"

This infuriates Steff beyond absolute control, and he runs around to my uncles' side of the car, again kicking, and kicking, and kicking.

Whilst my uncle sits there, laughing, and laughing, and laughing.

POLICE!

Steffs roars fill the air as he's wrestled to the ground, in a display of violence the likes of which the crowd of students as the bus stop have probably never seen before.

I just wanted to leave.
I didn't want any of this.

CHAPTER 19

It's about 8am, and I'm lying in bed, back at mums.

I hear her climbing the stairs, and I'm waiting on her shouting me to get up. But she passes by my bedroom door, and keeps walking along the hall.

I hear her opening my brothers bedroom door, and in a relaxing tone of voice she soothes "morning son, time to get up,"

Hmm. She sounds in a good mood.

Boom, boom, boom, boom.

What the fuck?

She's hammering her way back along the hall.

"AZARIA," She screeches, "GERRUP"

Every day I'm here is full of regret.

Bella, me and your gran (and uncle), have spoken about this exact moment a few times.
She thinks it's hilarious.
And, so did I, until I realised how fucked up it all really was.

CHAPTER 20

Dear Bella,

When your Grandad died, it turned out he had left a substantial amount of money, however it had all been left to your Gran, who said she "didn't need his money", and dutifully split it equally between me, your uncle, and your Grandads wife. She said it's what he would've wanted, and that he had left her the money regardless of the fact they had been divorced for years, because he knew she would do the right thing and make sure his kids got it.

I got £16,000, and your Uncle got £16,000.

Oh, wait, your Uncle got £16,000 and I got a few hundred.

Your Gran was, of course, in charge of the money, as your Uncle was 16, and me only 18 (with a crippling drug problem). She told us we could wait until your Uncle turned 21, and we get all the money to do as we please (as it wasn't fair if I got my share at 21, and he had to wait another 2 years).

Or we could put £8000 each into a business and the remainder of our money given to us in a monthly instalment of £200.

So, we put £8000 each into opening a Sweetie shop, which was all in your Grans name due to our young ages, but the premise was that the business was ours. A few months later, your Gran invested her own money into it, and we opened a second shop. It was all very successful.

But of course, I still had a raging smack habit. We opened the first shop in the summer of 2011, and after a few months I disappeared again, for just under a year. During this time, your Uncle still received his £200/month. Obviously, I wasn't there to get mine.

When I eventually got home, your Gran was driving us home from work one day, and we got talking about the money.

"Well, Tony got his, but you weren't here..." she shrugged.

My remaining half of my inheritance had been spent.

No big deal, I still owned some of the business. I thought.

Over the years, I came and went, I wasn't very stable. But after you, Bella, were born, I began working again on a regular basis. Out of the 11 years the shop/cafe had been open, I had been present for around 6.5. Take into account some of my disappearing stints only lasted a few months at a time.

When they decided to sell up, earlier on this year, I had been back working there regularly for 4 years.

They agreed to sell the business, and your Gran and Uncle were splitting the money between themselves.

I was speaking to my friend, telling her this, when she said, "Wait, Azaria, what about you?"

"What about me?"

"Didn't you put eight grand into that???"

Yes, but I hadn't always been there.

But, that's not really how money works... If I had placed that money into a bank, it would still be there.

"Right," my friend said, "even if you don't get any profit, surely you're entitled to your original investment?"

But I wasn't, because I was so young, everything was in your Grans name.

I remember sitting thinking, if I wasn't related, that I probably would've gotten my original investment.

I remember thinking, if I wasn't family, I would've gotten it, because I wouldn't have that family connection, and therefore wouldn't feel bad trying to claim it back through the small claims court. But, they knew I wouldn't do that. Wouldn't have a leg to stand on, because nothing was in writing. It wasn't my money, it never was, I had just been told it was.

So, your Uncle got his share, and blew it mostly on cannabis, the same thing he had done with his £200/month. Quite right! He was a young, single guy.

Your Gran paid off whatever she had to pay off.

And now, here I am, on Universal Credit, making between £20-£80/ month off the sale of my first book.

Bella, I have an ISA for you. It cannot be touched until you're 18, and you are the one that can access the money. I made sure of that when looking for a bank, that I couldn't access the money, so I wouldn't be tempted to "borrow" some when I'm skint, with the intention of putting it back.

And every time I find a copper, I put it into a jar, and tell you it's from Grandad. Hopefully before you turn 18, I've saved up enough coppers to give you that £8000.

I love you.

CHAPTER 21

Mum sat us down, and explained dad had £56,000 in a pension when he died. She explained to us that it was being split equally between me, my brother, and dads' wife, Rose.

She was only married to him for 3 fucking days, but cool. Mum wants to be "the bigger person", apparently. The money was legally left to her, even though they had been divorced for years, so she's entitled to it all. But no, she wants to be a noble, stand-up member of society.

"I never needed his money when he was alive, I don't need it now,"

I don't understand why a wife of 3 days is getting £17,000 of my dads' pension, that he started paying into in the 80s!!!

Bella, I kicked off. And was swiftly told to shut the fuck up. Rose wasn't happy with the £17,000 alone, so asked your gran for an extra £2000, which she took from me and your uncles' money. Rose claimed she needed the money to pay "inheritance tax". She told your gran she would pay it back.
But, she directly inherited sweet FUCK ALL.
And, that only ever applies if you directly inherit over £350,000.
But no, Azaria being Azaria, just being selfish, wants more money.
Did Rose pay the money back?
Did she fuck.
Anyway...

Mum said we could wait until my brother turns 21, and we both get the full amount each (apparently it would be unfair if I got it at 21, and he had to wait another 2 years. So, if we took that option, I would have to be the one that waits an extra 2 years).

Or, we can put £8000 each into starting up our own business, and she will give us the remaining £8000 in monthly instalments of £200.

We've decided on the business, that'll make us money in the long run.

And, we've came up with a great idea – an old-fashioned sweetie shop. How many of them do you see now? Like, proper old-fashioned sweetie shop, with all the old sweets in jars.

Fucking amazing idea. Brilliant.

We've decided on the name "Favers Candy Emporium", and we've found a wee shop to rent in Portobello High Street.

For the first time in my life, I feel like I've got a plan. A really good plan to get me moving forward.

Even if it fails, as a business, at least we tried.

CHAPTER 22

In the kitchen, I sit at the breakfast bar, eagerly writing away on a piece of paper.

We're gonna need an old sweetie supplier. Jars. Shelves. A till! Oh fuck, how could I forget about a till?

I'm alone, until I hear the front door open. Must be my mum and brother. That was quick.
They were meant to be painting the shop!

I turn around, and oh fuck – it's Billy.

Immediately my heart drops. He does nothing but make me feel like a cunt, but we seem to have come to an arrangement where we just ignore each other.

It's still awkward as fuck though.

"Awright hen," he smiles at me.

What the actual fuck?

I reply back meekly, "awright"

"Can I ask you a question?" He takes place on the opposite side of the breakfast bar, directly facing me.

This feels weird, but whatever, "Aye"

"What made you get back with him? Are you no sick of the shite yet?"

I'm totally taken aback, I feel like this is a trap, to start an argument or something. I feel like saying "Yous all fucking know why! Because I've never been welcome here!"

Instead, I say, "...I dunno, to be honest. It started with us arranging to meet up for a bit of fun, and just snowballed…"

"Surely you knew how it would end up though?" He questions.

I shrug.

He opens his arms wide, and with a smile, confidently tells me, "You should know, if you ever want to suck dick, you come to me"

CHAPTER 23

I'm shaking, I can't stop shaking.

In between the palms of my hands is a serrated knife. I had been using it to get out bits of weed that were stuck in my grinder, and now I'm sitting on my bed, with it in my hands as my entire body convulses with anxiety.

If this cunt - this dirty, smelly, baldy, CUNT - Billy, walks into this room, this knife is getting imbedded right in the centre of his fucking forehead!!!

I can't believe he's just asked me to suck his fucking dick!

All sorts of shit is running through my mind.

How long has he felt like this about me? He's been in my life since I was fucking 9!

How could he do this to my mum?

If he's gonna cheat, why with his wifes daughter!?

But, worst of all... Who the fuck is actually going to believe me?
Who's gonna believe the smackheed that has trouble following her around wherever she goes?

Bella, I eventually told your gran 3 years later, when she announced they were divorcing and I felt I had nothing to lose. She believed me, she said, but asked me to keep it quiet. I done as I was told. She said nobody else in the family would believe me, she didn't want to get caught in the middle defending me, apparently.
Turns out, her believing me didn't actually make a blind bit of difference – she got back with him a couple of months after I told her.

CHAPTER 24

The sweetie shop has been a hit, it's done so well. Portobello is a really tight-knit community, and they have welcomed us in with open arms. It's good to have a fresh start, basically. I mean, it's not like any of the customers know me, or what I've done in the past.

All they know is that I'm a young business owner trying to make it, alongside my brother. The whole "we opened this business with our dads inheritance money" is a fucking good gimmick – it pulls on peoples heartstrings and brings them in as customers.

Again, it's just nice to feel and be normal, and have people know me as Azaria, the sweetie shop lassie.

That image didn't last long. My first relapse back on to gear after opening the shop, your Gran made it her duty to inform every customer that asked where I was that I was a raging Heroin addict.
"Well, you have to be honest with people when they ask where you are..."
All that honesty done was make it clear to every customer that I actually didn't have a say in the business, realistically. They all seen me as just another junkie.
But it's okay, because your gran stepped in and saved the day by joining the business.
It soon became your grans business, even with mine and your uncles' surname on the door.
People would come in, ask me or your uncle if they could speak to the owner, we would let them know that was either one of us, and their reply always was "I'll just wait on your mum..."
So, the whole "this is the kids' business they run with their dads inheritance" REALLY was just a big bullshit gimmick to get people in the door. The entire time in Portobello was spent bullshitting people.

It's the end of the day, and I'm alone, starting to cash up. As soon as I open the till, I notice it is suspiciously light. I don't understand how it could be, it can't be. It really can't be. It's not like any customers have access to the till, or if they did – we would have noticed. 100%.

It can't be short. It must just look that way.

I start counting. 12345678910. That's £10, put it to the side. 12345678910. So that's £20, put it to the side.

I continue counting the money, sweat beginning to form on my forehead as I count and count and realise that, it's not just short – it's REALLY fucking short.

The float is meant to be £100. But once I take out the profits for the day, there's only a £20 float.

I want to cry.
My brothers at it again.

Bella, I think your uncle is a kleptomaniac, seriously. That guy has stolen, and stole, and stole, so brazenly. And every time he was forgiven and it swept under the rug.
If it was me, I would've been carted out the door by the collar and told to find somewhere else to live.

This has been going on too long now. I've been noticing the till has been short, but only ever £15 at the most. And, of course, genuine mistakes are made, so I brought it up to mum, but didn't go off on one. She told me to keep an eye.

And now here I am, standing with only £20 to put back into the till as a float. And no fucking wages.

Your uncle continued thieving up until I was pregnant with you, when he spent almost £1000 I had saved up for you. His partner at the time tried to defend it by saying "but look at everything you've stolen, Azaria", and I almost fell out of my chair.
I was rarely home to fucking steal!!!
And with all due respect, the twice I did steal from family, in 10 years, was nothing compared to his daily/weekly thefts.

You know, like the thefts that resulted in them almost losing the business completely, because he spent everything on cocaine.

I just don't know what to do. I don't want to even bring it up to mum, because she'll just make excuses and I'll just get angry. But I need fucking wages.

This is what I don't understand – he got his wages today, too. So, there was literally NO reason for him to steal £80!

He blew it on weed, Bella, the usual.

CHAPTER 25

My throat's burning, between this joint and laughing, it's on fire.

Steff is lying in a heap next to me, laughing hysterically. We're watching South Park.

Fuck, I know I shouldn't be back here. But I am. I really think things have changed with him.

Once mum came into our business, we started renting another shop in the Grassmarket, so right in the city centre, and 5 minutes away from Steffs flat. I knew it wouldn't be long before we were back together.
Plus, I kind of know that if I didn't get back with him, I'd be in for a hard time in this new shop. I could see the windows getting smashed for knocking him back, so I agreed to meet him again. And here we are now.

It's not too bad though, he's actually got a job.
He sorted out his CSCS card, and got a job labouring at the Primark being built on Princes Street. He's getting like £600 a week! Not bad at all.

But he seems to still ask me for money, too, for gear. I only get £150 a week but I if I don't give him the money then I feel so bad. He reminds me of all the times he's went out shoplifting in the mornings, whilst I've been lying in my bed, or all the times he's sold gear.

I never remind him that he never actually sold gear, or dealt anything. He would buy a bigger bit, sort it out into tenner bags, not get a single sale, and then ask me for the money to cover it because he had smoked it all, with me only getting a bag or 2 out of 20.

Regardless, things have been okay. We haven't argued at all, and things are good.

We've got a tenner bag left for in the morning, but we decide to smoke it now. Neither of us start actually rattling until around 12pm, so we should be okay in the morning sorting out another bit. I can nip out of the shop on a "break" to come for a burn. Nobody will know.

He's not working this weekend, so that's the plan.

"I love you baby," he tells me, "I'm glad we've sorted aw this shite out"

I look at him, and smile, I'm so happy. I really think we can make a go of things now, we've both got jobs and seem to be working together.

"I love you too"

CHAPTER 26

No, no, no, no, no, no!

Fucking NO!!!!!!!!

"Why didn't you wake me up!?" I cry to Steff, as he lies there.

"You just looked so peaceful, like you needed the sleep," he smiles.

"But the fucking shop, Steff!"

I look at my phone. Umpteen missed calls and texts. I can't bring myself to read them, I genuinely just can't do it. I know it's gonna be full of abuse.

And to top it off, it's fucking 1pm... So, we're rattling! I can't go into work rattling, we smoked that last tenner bag we were supposed to keep for the morning, and now we don't have money, and I won't get wages, obviously!

Steff begins to get ready, "looks like we'll need to go for a shoplift"

He looks surprisingly calm and happy considering I've pretty much just fucked over everything with the shop.

But he's right, we're rattling and need to go for a shoplift.

I switch my phone off. They'll take the hint.

It's not like my family give an actual fuck about me anyway.

CHAPTER 27

I'm so, so tired of this shoplifting pish already.

I've only been back at Steffs full-time for the last week, and I'm so sick already.

It's not like I can go home, though, is it?

I don't know what to do.

Suicide is genuinely getting more tempting as the days go on.

I promise I won't make it past 2012. *I promise.*

CHAPTER 28
PART 1

"HARRISON"

"HARRISON"

"HAAAAAAARISOOOOOON"

Bzzbzzbzzbzzbzz-bzz-bzzzz.

Who the fuck is at the buzzer at 2am? Who the fuck is shouting up on Steff?

Oh, why am I even questioning myself, it's *obviously* Stuart. He's the only person that acknowledges Steff by his surname, Harrison.

Bella, for you and the readers benefit, I'm going to remind you that Stuart is Steffs friend from the start of book 1, the one that gave me my first few lines of gear.

I can't be arsed with this cunt! I seriously can't be fuckin' arsed with him!
Any time he comes up he ends up well overstaying his welcome. Claiming he'll come out shoplifting with us, then actually doing fuck all but escort us shoplifting, but we're still sitting sharing our food, tobacco, smack, and weed with him, like a pair of fucking dingles. And Steff won't say a damn thing to him about it, all he'll do is take it out on me when we're alone.

To be honest, this is the first time in my life I'm starting to see Steff differently, I don't know what it is, I can't put my finger on it. But I'm really starting to notice that he is far from this big, scary hard-man he makes himself out to be.

My doctor has been prescribing me Zopiclone, to help me sleep, and it makes me so, so groggy. I ain't getting out of my bed to let him in!

Steff obviously does though, and as I turn over in bed to avoid the light from the hall shining through the crack in the bedroom door, I hear the muffled voices of Steff and Stuart.

What the fuck are they doing in the hallway?

Why is Steff putting his shoes on?

Aw, fuck knows man, back to sleep.

Bams.

CHAPTER 28
PART 2

For fuck sake!
Will this pair of dafties keep it down!?
What the fuck are they banging so hard up the stairs for?

The bedroom wall runs alongside the communal stair, and I can hear Steff & Stuart pounding along our landing like a herd of elephants. I'm raging, it's probably like 3am at this point, now, I dunno how long they've been out for.

Cold air hits every one of my nerves that are outside of the covers as the front door is swung open and quickly closed so hard the vibrations shake the bedroom door.

What the fuck is going on?

They sound like they're panicking over something.
They sound like they're really panicking.

Nah, that's not right. I'm getting up.

Oh my god. Zopiclone makes me ridiculously groggy, seriously, I'm having to fight my own eyelids to open them even halfway.

I wrap the duvet around me, so my partially naked body is covered, and I shuffle through to the hall. Both of them are standing there frozen in position as soon as I appear in the doorway, looking at me like a deer in headlights. They've both got blood on them, although between the two of them, Stuart is covered. His trainers look like he's just walked straight through the 9 circles of Hell.

You know what? I don't even want to fucking know.

Seriously, I don't want to know. Because if I know, then I KNOW, and I don't want whatever the fuck it is on my conscience. Fuck it.

I turn back around, and go to bed.

When I said I don't want to know, I was being 100% serious.

CHAPTER 29

BANGBANGBANG.

The banging jolts me awake.

WHAT THE FUCK IS IT NOW?

As I stand up, they bang the door again.

The police bang the door again, slightly harder this time.

So, where the fuck is Steff?
And Stuart?
How the fuck is it 11am!?

"JUST A MINUTE, I'M TRYING TO GET CLOTHES ON!" I shout back.

Looking for a top to put on, my eyes scan the room, and doing so – out the window. The street outside is taped off.

I'm shaking like a leaf, and answer the door, before they bang again as if I've no already heard them and shouted back.

Opening the door is like a slap into reality, as standing there on the doorstep is two police – murder squad – in white hazmat suits.

"We're just doing door-to-door enquiries," the male begins, "did you hear anything last night at all?"

My response is immediate, "no, I was in my bed."

They quickly ask for my details, which I give. As soon as the doors closed, it's like someone pushes a button on my body that begins a vibration-like process; first my arms start shaking, then as I get into the living room my legs start, when I chest down my chest starts heaving as if I'm crying, but I'm not.
Where the fuck is Steff? What the fuck's going on?

As time passes, my anxiety worsens. I keep an eye on the situation unfolding outside, and it's getting worse – gradually, over the next hour or so, more police turn up, and a private ambulance. The shaking doesn't stop.

Jeremy Kyle shouting at some poor jobseeker on national TV is interrupted by the bang of the landing door, and a couple of guys voices. I pray it's Steff, but after a few seconds, when the door doesn't open, it becomes clear it's not him. Fuck.

But then why are there guys voices talking outside of the door!?

The panic gets even worse, and I didn't think that was possible. I'm expecting the door to get smashed in by the police, with their big red key, any minute now.

I bet they're waiting on an entry warrant!

The noise of mental clangs takes over all the noise on the landing. I can't sit here anymore, but I don't want to check the peephole in case they happen to put the door in at the same time. Fuck, what a dilemma.

Surely, if they were gonna put the door in, they would've done it by now?

Fuck this, I can't sit here! I need to see what the noise is.

I creep through to the hall to ensure they absolutely cannot hear me moving about behind the door, and lean against the top half of the door, looking out of the peephole.

Why do they have ladders? I squint as I watch a policeman shuffling around the landing with a set of ladders over his shoulder. *What the fuck are they doing?*

Doing everything I can to control the volume of my breathing, the entire right side of my face stays plastered to the door, as through the peephole I watch the police carefully push the ladders out of the landing window, onto the tiny balcony, and then use them to climb up onto the small bit of exposed roof over our flat.

They're looking for a fucking murder weapon!!!

This is so, so fucking bad.

The internal panic instantly becomes external, and I suddenly don't give a flying fuck if they hear me move away from the door.

I can't believe this shit. I can't fucking believe it.

"BABE," His voice shouting up to the window from outside is clear.

I open the window, "WHAT?"

He's with 3 people who know, I'm assuming they've just all scored.

"COME DOON,"

"I CAN'T! NOBODIES ALLOWED TO LEAVE THE HOUSE,"

He quickly speaks to the policeman standing at the front door to the stair and shouts back up that I've been given the okay to leave the building.

When I open the landing door, a policeman warns me not to touch anything, and escorts me down the stairs, and out of the flats. The whole way down there is policemen and women, in forensic suits, combing every single inch of the building with brushes and clear tape.

Leaving the building, I run into Steffs arms, as he tells me he's sorted us out for the day, and all of the shit that's taken place earlier in the day immediately leaves my brain as the realisation I'm gonna have a good time getting high hits me.

Yesssss.

CHAPTER 30

Steff is awfully calm considering the situation.

Maybe he didn't have anything to do with it?

As we start walking away from the building, I look up to see if I can see what neighbour it is that's died.

Straight away I see the police in the flat underneath the flat that's directly under us, on the 3rd floor.
Lewis – the vallie dealer.

You know what? Not even remotely surprised. Whether or not Steff did have anything to do with it, I ain't surprised that it's Lewis that's been the victim of whatever *this* is.

The whole way along the road I feel very weird. I can't explain it. Like I'm in a dream, as in I physically feel like I'm in a dream. I don't feel like I'm walking, I feel like I'm levitating alongside Steff as we make our way to his pals' house, as the pals' girlfriend – Jennifer – makes small talk with me the entire way along.

At Dalry, we turn into a wee scheme that sits at the back of the big Co-Op.
Funny, it's almost *always* immediately obvious what flat we're heading up to when we turn into a street for the first time.

Towels for curtains? A broken outer panel on the window?
Definitely a junkie house.

Getting into the house is like Takeshis Castle, a real-life smackhead assault course. All 5 of us squeeze through the hallway in a single file, dodging cardboard boxes, sharps containers on top of the cardboard boxes, fuck, why is there so many cardboard boxes?

See, Bella, back then, there was absolutely no excuse for the amount of cardboard these people stored in their home – Amazon Prime did not exist.

I think these people are incorporating cardboard into their diet, there's so much of it. I think their entire life is cardboard-based. I'm very surprised there isn't a box in the corner with a screen drawn on it, like a television. *A cardboard television.*

WHY is there so much cardboard in here!?

In the living room, I'm offered a seat, which I accept. I shuffle a load of cardboard off a space on the couch... And then instantly sit down on top of another pile of cardboard.

I'm paranoid about smoking in here, if the head falls off the cigarette, then the whole place will go up. A box of matches is actually *LESS* flammable than this entire flat.

An entire conversation is taking place in the background as I sit on my cardboard throne, admiring the cardboard surroundings. *Beautiful.*

WHY!? Seriously... Why is there so much!?

"Here, babe," Steff nudges me, and hands me the tooter, "in your own world there, aye?"

Aye, a fucking cardboard one.

CHAPTER 31

Once the gear was smoked, we left the cardboard house to head to the big Co-Op in Dalry – it's an absolute piece of piss to steal from, because:

- They only put security tags on the bottles at the front of the shelves.

- All of their spirits are out on full display, for anyone to grab.

- There's 2 exits from the shop, and one of them doesn't have security gates.

- The security guard goes on an hour break, between 7pm-8pm.

It's 7:10pm, so we've got plenty time, we might even have enough time to go in twice, because the shop we sell the alcohol to is only across the road, and through the Dalry tunnel.

I fucking hate shoplifting. I have no idea how Steff can do it so fucking calmly, like he can just walk into a shop without a care in the world. When I walk into a shop, my heart pounds so, so hard that I can feel certain veins pulsing, like on my hands, or forehead. I feel sick.

But there's times I feel less sick than others, and this is one of those times, because I know security is on his break.

Getting into the shop is easy, and we take great care not to be seen by any staff, regardless of how confidently we've strolled in. It's not hard to stay undetected at this time in the evening though, most staff are on the tills, serving customers, because it's so busy.

The drink aisle is busy when we get there, so we wait a couple of minutes to let other customers leave, and it's not long before they do. But we aren't psychic, and we don't know when the next customer will walk into the aisle, so the second it's clear we start quickly (and quietly) piling bottles of Jack Daniels into our bags.

Jack Daniels is an awkward shape, but they're smaller than big bottles of vodka, and it's expensive. So, we get more for a 70cl of Jack Daniels than we would with a 70cl of Smirnoff vodka.

As soon as I put bottle number 5 into my bag, a woman walks into the aisle. Time to go.

Walking out is just as easy as walking in.

I can't believe we keep getting away with stealing from this shop! We've been hitting it almost daily, because it's so easy.

In total we got 11 bottles, and that's £110. I can't wipe the smile off my face as the Pakistani shop owner hands over 5 £20 notes and 10 pound coins. I have the biggest smile on my face, I really do.

I'm smiling because it's a relief that we, not only got something, but we got a lot. Enough to get a teinth for tonight, and a half for the morning.

And then, as we walk back along the long stretch of road, from Fountainpark to Tollcross, Steff brings up the neighbour, and I make a comment about the victim constantly pissing people off.

"He's always got somecunt shouting up at his window, calling him a junkie," I remind Steff.
"Aye, but they aren't calling him a Junkie," he informs me, "that's his nickname!"
I scrunch my face up, "surely no?"
"Haha, aye!" He's laughing, "swear to god, babe, he's known as Junkie."

And then it suddenly makes sense that every time I've heard people shouting up to the guys window, multiple times a day, that never once have any of the people shouting had even an inclination of aggression in their voices. They've been shouting up "Junkie", just shouting on their pal, or dealer...

"Am no surprised, the cunt had a stinkin' attitude anyway," Steff scoffs, "he knocked Stuart back for tick, just being a dick, with that powder-power shite."

When the fuck was Stuart knocked back for tick? He doesn't live in Edinburgh; he only shows up every now and again at our flat. When the fuck did Steff and Stuart go and see this guy for tick?

Penny drops.
Actually, I'm gonna stop thinking about it now, I just want a burn.

A policeman standing on patrol outside of the building, asks us our names, and what flat we're in. Don't know why he bothered, it's not like he checked anything to make sure we live there.

A female officer escorts us up to the flat, and when we get in, we don't even bother taking shoes or jackets off – tinfoil is more important. We need a burn.

I don't know what to do.

CHAPTER 32

Days like these are the best, seriously.

We've woke up with a half-teinth, and not only that – it's payday. Thank fuck for employment and support allowance.

I always thought it was gonna be a hard job getting onto ESA, because I'm fit for work. Turns out it was a case of walking into the doctors office and telling them I wasn't fit for work and getting a sick note. It's a lot harder now, trust me.

I'm about half-way down a line on the foil, with the tooter in my mouth, when we are rudely interrupted by loud banging.

Me and Steff immediately make eye contact.

That's the fucking police.

What the fuck do they want? Me and Steff have already spoken to them, albeit briefly, but we're the same as the other neighbours – we don't know anything about this shite.

I motion to Steff to answer the door, and his eyes grow bigger as he shakes his head aggresively.

I whisper-hiss at him, "why!?"

He doesn't answer me, just puts his arm out in front of me to stop me from moving, and I don't understand why. Don't get me wrong, I don't know why we need to be spoken to, but I don't know why Steff isn't answering – he's making us look dodgy!

It's a good 10 minutes before the banging stops, but we know the police are still there; if they had left, we would have heard the landing door open, and shut, and then footsteps down the stairs, or the lift. They're pretending they've went away, assuming we will start jumping about and making noise, thus proving we are home.

Not today, fuckers.
Yous can fuck right off.

It's another 10 minutes before we hear the landing door move and walking down the stair. Finally. But we are still paranoid that they are somehow still hanging about, so we finish smoking our gear as quietly as we can.

Bella, you totally underestimate how loud tinfoil is until you need to use it in silence.

We're still whispering, and I quietly start firing questions at Steff.

Why didn't you answer?
You do know that'll make us look dodgy?
Are you radge?
How are we gonna leave here to go and score?
What the fuck are we gonna do?

He tells me that the reason he isn't answering is because him and Stuart were in the house the same night the neighbour was murdered, but he swears he had nothing to do with it. He tells me that they asked for Valium on tick, and didn't get it, there was a bit of an argument and then they left.

"Am gonna look suspicious either way, Azaria!" he stresses, "if I don't tell the polis I was there, and they find out, they'll think a done it. But if a tell them me and Stuart did go down, they'll just assume we've done it 'cause of our criminal records."

Makes sense.
Kind of.

CHAPTER 33

Days have passed and we've managed to avoid police, but I don't know how. They keep coming to the door, and I don't think Steff realises just how suspicious it looks every time they come to the door and we ignore it, even though it's obvious we're home.

It's been one of those shitty days. Nearly got caught shoplifting bottles of wine in Sainsburys, the manager pretty much caught us, but a customer asked him a question and that opened up a 1-second window of opportunity for me to leave.

Don't ever take your eyes off a shoplifter, they don't just get away, but they will also steal even more stock on their way out the door.

Steff blamed me for almost getting caught, I don't know why, it's not like I can control when and where people walk! I asked him to explain how it was my fault, and rather than give me a response he just spun around and punched me full-force right in the solar-plexus. It took the wind out of me completely, and I spent the rest of the walk to the shop silently sobbing.

Our normal dealers didn't have, so we went around to another dealers house in Dalry – an older couple. The wife, Denise, used to be completely "normal", never touched a drug in her life, she was a big bank manager for the Bank of Scotland.
*Then she developed sciatica, and at the time, the doctor put her on Methadone for pain relief. This was during the eighties when there wasn't **that** much research on methadone, it's withdrawal, and what it done to people.*
She was on Methadone for 4 years, when they just decided to stop prescribing it. It was the first time she had ever felt any kind of withdrawal. She took a week off work, told a friend, who told her the

best way to stop the withdrawal was with Heroin.
Now it's over 2 decades later, and her and her husband are raging heroin addicts, selling as much gear as they can to pay off the dealers from Liverpool they tried to bump (who subsequently travelled up from Liverpool, and set their house on fire).

When we get in the house, the husband, Robbie, greets me with a smile, "hello gorgeous!"
"How you doin', Robbie?" I ask him, sitting down between him and Denise, as he starts weighing out our bit on the scales.

As he passes Steff the foil, offering us a free charge, he also hands us both a couple of Valium each. Blues, 10mg.
"They're the real deal," he ensures us, not that it matters because the pills were travelling down to our stomachs at the point he tells us.

It soon becomes clear they are not real though, because they are kicking in with the strength of an Ox, and so fast. So, so fast.

Now I'm sitting sideways, and I'm slurring my words.

This is fucking great.

CHAPTER 34

Valium prevents your brain from creating new memories – maybe that's why I can't remember us getting home?

Sitting on the couch, passing the tooter back and forth between each other, it's like the Valium has brought us both deeper and deeper into a timeline where we are both so open, full of happiness and amazing ideas, and unlimited love for each other. It's times like these that I realise he truly loves me, because I know Valium can make him angry, so if he's managing to keep his anger at bay then it's because he cares for me.

Don't, don't even try and work that out. I was blind, with a capital B.

As the night goes on, our conversations turn much more serious. We've stop talking about all the happy shit that may or may not (probably not) happen for us in the future. Up until now it's been a word salad of ridiculously high expectations for our lives, considering we are a pair of shoplifting heroin-addicts.

Steff asks me what's the worst thing I ever done. And I don't really have an answer, I don't. I don't think there's anything that bad I've done.
I tell him about Billy coming on to me, and he's furious. He asks why I haven't told my mum, why I didn't tell her immediately, and I remind him that – duh – it's fucking me.

He agrees they wouldn't believe me.

He burns me another couple of lines, and I struggle to stay straight the whole way down the foil, I'm swaying from side to side. As I hold in the smoke, I fire back the same question as him.

His expression changes from not-bothered-about-anything, to

pure serious, he won't look away from me.

"You can't tell ANYONE Azaria, I swear to fuck," He slurs his words a bit, "Seriously, I don't think you understand, you canny tell anybody."

I take the foil away from him, and lean over in my sitting position, so my face is right under his, and I beg him. I promise him, and promise him, and promise him, I won't tell.

"Listen, if I tell you and you tell ANYONE. If ANYTHING happens, I'll know it's came from *you*,"

I take the threat on the chin, that's fine.

"Lewis didny get done in with a hammer, that's a load of shite," he refers to the police searching all of the bins in the area for a weapon and the rumours, "Stuart jumped on his heed."

I can't speak.
Like I physically feel sick.

"See! This is why a didny want to tell you Azaria!" He places his face into his hands, "if this comes out, even if it wasn't you, it's *you* that's getting done!"

He starts turning slightly aggressive, and I start turning into the version of myself that begs and pleads for him to calm down, that version of myself that will do ANYTHING not to get hurt.

I'm stuttering and can't really get words out through the tears. I just keep begging.

"Am no gonna hurt you!" he snaps at me, "but if Stuart gets done for it then he's no gonna stop until you're where Lewis is!!!"

No, no, no.

I wish I had just kept to not knowing.

Things calm down a bit, I do the whole begging-thing that Steff genuinely seems to enjoy so much, and he continues to "make sure" I won't say anything.

When he's sure I won't say anything, he goes into detail.

They went down for some Valium, but Lewis kicked off because it was so late in the night, and he ended up getting punched about. When he fell to the ground, Stuart – who is 6'4" and big-build – jumped on his head with all his weight.

"The blood hit the ceiling," Steff shakes his head.

CHAPTER 35

Waking up and lifting my head off the pillow feels like a task for the worlds strongest man. I hate valium-hangovers.

There's mostly silence as we get up, and start getting ready to go out for a shoplift.

On the way to our first stop, Tesco, Steff asks me if I remember what he said last night, and I tell him yes.

"Fuck, I was hoping you didn't,"

CHAPTER 36

We got a puppy!

Steff got a phone call from his dad, asking if we wanted a puppy. She's a rottweiler crossed with a Labrador, she's gorgeous. Her name is Molly.

I know people might think it's a stupid idea, but honestly, I think this dog could really help us. Steff adores her, it's like seeing him with a newborn baby. I'm so happy.

Bella, the dog was just another thing he could aim his aggression at.

"Molly!" I shout, "Look at mummy!"

She sits right up next to Steff on the couch, and I take a photo.

I love this dog.

CHAPTER 37

It's been a very bad day today – we've been in umpteen shops, and just can't get a shoplift.

We've got Molly with us, so she's been tied up outside of the shops whilst we've been inside, massively failing at shoplifting.

Finally, we get into the wee Sainsburys up at Morningside, and I manage to get a few bottles of wine into my bag. Unfortunately, the manager popped up, out of nowhere, so I couldn't get any more.

Half-way down the road to our usual shop to sell our stuff, and we get into an argument about me not being able to get any more bottles from Sainsburys.

"If I took anymore, I would've got caught!" I try my hardest to explain.

He rolls his eyes, "aye, okay Azaria. More like you just didn't bother!"

Why the fuck would I not bother?
I'm rattling just as much as you!

Without hesitation, in the middle of the argument, Steff seems to lose all control, and without even considering whether there's people around us, he boots Molly in the stomach as hard as he can.

Her yelp echoes through the street.

I audibly gasp, and Steff tells me to shut the fuck up.

And suddenly, I regret us getting this dog, because she's just an extra target.

CHAPTER 38

I don't know why I've done this.

Seriously, I don't know why I've done this to myself. I don't know why I got back with him.

I dunno what has happened, but now he is never nice to me, at all. Ever.

From the moment he wakes up, until the moment he goes to bed, the level of abuse I receive is incredible, no matter what I do.

Even when the day goes as planned, and we don't have any problems shoplifting, he still finds something to rip into me about.

Walking home, after a long day of stealing, selling, scoring, and repeating that a couple of times, I'm exhausted. We've got our gear, our foil, our tobacco, but I just want to sleep, I'm so fucking tired.

"Slag," I hear Steff whisper at the back of me.

"Whore," he whispers again, and I assume he's taking the piss.

I turn around, "haha, very funny Steff."

"What are you talking about?" He looks at me, seemingly confused.

"I heard you, calling me a slag,"

He starts laughing, and tells me I'm hearing things. I turn back around.

"Slag," another whisper, "slag."

"Slag,"

"Tramp,"

"Dirty,"

I eventually turn back around, "right Steff, we get the point, very funny."

He explodes, "WHAT ARE YOU FUCKIN TALKIN' ABOOT?"

I... I don't know what tp say.
100% he was whispering names to me.

He snarls in my face that he didn't call me anything, and backhanders me.

We walk home in silence, with him occasionally whispering that I'm a slag.

CHAPTER 39

Fuck.

I'm lying in bed, and I just know that we've woken up too late.

I don't know what to do, seriously. All of the security guards will have started their shifts by now, and I now Steff will somehow blame me for sleeping in.

So, I lie there, too scared to move.

At least, if he thinks he wakes up first, he might blame himself. Even if he doesn't blame himself, at least he won't blame me.

I lie there. Silent. Scared to move.
Yet, I'm trying to appreciate this silence, because I know it won't last long.

An hour passes. Molly starts moaning to get out. It's his morning to take her out, but I bet he won't remember that.

Her moaning becomes louder, as she nudges his hand with her nose.

Before I can't open my eyes, he explodes.

"YOU DIRTY FUCKING BASTARD," he's screaming at Molly, who is now cowering in the corner.

I jump out of the bed, naked, "Steff! What the fuck are you doing!?"

I'm halfway over the bed when he starts pummelling into the dog with lefts and rights, using his fists to make sure he hits every single rib in her body.

I'm screaming, "STOP!!!"

"PLEASE STOP!"

"STEFF...PLEASE STOP!"

It's genuinely like he's in a trance, he just keeps beating fuck out of this dog, so I must utilise what I know is the very last resort – using myself as a human shield.

I throw myself in front of Molly, but he's so hyped-up he doesn't even realise – he just keeps hammering away with his fists.

And then he does realise it's me. Oh, for fuck sake.

He stops.

And he places his hand on my head, making sure he grips as much hair as he can.

He pulls me up off of Molly by the handful of hair, and before I can react, he uses all of his strength to push me back down to the floor.

And he rubs my face in the dogs piss.

As soon as he's done smooshing my face into the urine-soaked carpet, he drops my head, and I'm that exhausted I just let it drop and smash my face off the ground again.

He's in the bathroom, and I can hear him cursing, calling em and the dog every name under the sun.

I need to get out of here.

I fling my clothes on as quickly as possible, and without a second thought I leave the flat. I'm going to mum.

And, as I knew she would, she comes to collect me.

As I get in the car, and put my seatbelt on, she asks what happened, and I explain.

"Well," she begins, "no wonder he fucking hits you Azaria, with you're shouting, do you have any idea how loud you are?"

I have no reply, I genuinely don't.

She starts the car up, and instead of driving east, the way home, she turns back around.

She wanted to make sure Steff was okay, Bella. Of course she did.

We pull in to Steffs building, and there's minimal conversation as we make our way in to and up the stairs. She's adamant she's taking Molly, even though I've told her he won't let us take the dog.

Steff answers the door.

"Are you alright, Steff?" my mum asks him, "do you want us to take Molly?"

He shakes his head.

"Do you need any money? For food? Electric?"

Yes, Bella. You are reading this correctly.
It was this exact moment I realised I was truly on my own in this world.

CHAPTER 40

I don't know why I do this to myself.

I don't know why I come "home".

I just don't fucking know.

We're into 2013, and things haven't changed a fucking bit. The only thing that has changed is the fact that my mum left her job with British Gas, put money into Favers Candy Emporium, and opened another shop up down at the Grassmarket.

5 minutes away from Steff.

And I feel like she has me working in that shop specifically on purpose.

She does. Because this shop makes more money, and me – the heroin addict – is apparently more trustworthy than my sticky-fingered brother.

But I still get treated like a junkie.

This stint back home only lasted a few weeks, Bella, before I fucked them all off again and went back to Steff.
Because, honestly, compared to your Granny – Steff was the lesser of two evils.

CHAPTER 41

So, what happened with the Grassmarket?

Well, your Granny put the same amount in as me and your uncle to open the shop, but as with the Portobello shop, it became very clear that the shop wasn't mine, nor your uncles. Even though we caught the attention of BBC news, who ran a story about the "poor kids that used their dads inheritance to open up this business."

But ultimately, it wasn't ours.

Anyway, after a few months of the Grassmarket shop being open, your Granny decided it was a splendid idea to let her best friends' husband – who was literally <u>BRAIN DAMAGED</u> (yes, he was physically and permanently brain damaged because of a stroke)– buy into the business as another owner.

Within a couple of weeks, she seen how grave a mistake that actually was.

He strolled into the business like he had always been a part of it, started trying to call big shots, and berating anything me or your uncle done.

One day, he asked me to fill jars, which I done. It took me no longer than 10 minutes. This pissed him off, and he phoned your granny "I don't think Azaria is filling the jars right!" He then went and "checked" the jars to make sure I had filled them, and then the next day when I came in, he apologised.

Sorry... What the actual FUCK is that about?

On New Years Day, the busiest day of the year, he forgot to put a crucial lollipop order in. So instead of making over a grand easily in that one day, we made only just over a hundred.

It just got worse and worse, to the point your gran just wanted shot of him, so she gave him the option to buy us out, and take the Grassmarket shop for himself, because if things kept going the way they were going we were all going to lose not only the Grassmarket shop, but the Portobello shop, too.

So, that was that.

The grassmarket shop is still open, being run by him, which surprised me, but I'd imagine my mums ex-best friend (his wife) is doing all of the "business" work.

It was a shame because, to be honest, he's actually a nice guy. But you know what they say about mixing friends with business – DON'T DO IT!

CHAPTER 42

I don't know what the fuck has happened, but I've only been back at Steffs a couple of weeks, and for whatever reason he has just upped the ante on this bullshit.

Every single day is the same. Literally every day.

Maybe two or three days out of 7, I'm awakened in the morning by being physically thrown from the bed, or a random slap, purely because he's woken up in a bad mood. But every day he wakes up in a bad mood. Every fucking day.

It's not going to be long before I kill myself. I can't do this anymore.

And it's either he kills me, or I kill myself. And I don't want to give the cunt the satisfaction.

This morning is no different from the others, except instead of being thrown out of the bed by him pushing me, today he feels the need to stand up out of the bed, and flip the mattress from his side, resulting in me being thrown out from my side, and rolling into the wall at full speed.

"What the fuck was that for!?" I cry, lying in a crumpled heap on the floor.

"FUCKING SHUT IT, BITCH," He sneers as he uses his index finger to aggressively point at me.

I shut it.

He starts putting his clothes on to go for a shoplift, and I know if I don't get up, and follow quickly behind him, things will get worse.

He storms out of the flat before I can put my shoes on, so I must run after him to catch up. He does this on purpose, it's like he loves me physically chasing them.

Finally catching up to him, we quickly nip into the Tesco Express at Fountainbridge, and fill our bags full of chocolate and coffee.

On the way along to the shop to sell the stuff, I'm a few steps ahead of Steff.

He whispers, "slag."

"Slag," he whispers again, "dirty."

I ignore it, and it continues.

"Slag,"

"Slag,"

"Whore,"

"Slaggy pants,"

"Slag,"

I eventually turn around, "Right then, ha-ha, very funny."

"What the fuck are you talking about? You're fuckin insane by the way," he insists I'm nuts.

This continues along the road, and I ask him twice more to stop, both times he laughs at me and tells me I'm a fucking schizo. The third time I ask him to stop, he punches me.

After that, I would just let him call me the names. Every single time we were outside, he would do it. And I mean every single time we went out, he would purposely walk behind me whispering insults. If I ever dared challenge him about it, I got a backhander.

CHAPTER 43

I really, really can't fucking do this anymore, I want to die.

Earlier on he battered me from the front door, all the way to the kitchen, because I didn't hang up on time in the phone box, our dealers phone went to voicemail and it swallowed all the phone money, so we didn't have any more change for a second call.
As soon as the voicemail came on, I realised I had made a mistake by not being faster.

Mow we've had to dip into our gear money, I'm a fucking idiot. I can't believe I didn't hang up quickly enough, no wonder he battered me!

I'm always amazed when I look in the mirror after a slap and see there's no marks. He always seems to punch or kick my actual head, or my body. I don't think he's ever given me a proper black eye before. But he's left plenty of bruises elsewhere, just where nobody else really can see.

Stepping out of the shower, the buzzer goes, and I know it's him. He went back out himself to score, after coming back up to the flat to smash me and get some change for another call.

When he walks in, I'm on the couch. I don't know what to say. In fact, I do – nothing. I darent speak after he's hit me, he's made it clear I can only speak when spoken to.

"Awright babe?" He chirps as he sorts the tinfoil out, as if nothing has happened.

I nod.

But inside I scream "I WANT TO DIE!"

CHAPTER 44

I can't do this anymore. Like, I really can't fucking do this anymore.

But I'm so scared to die.

It's me or him.

He's lying next to me on the bed sleeping, and as I watch over him, I feel an anger boiling inside of me, the likes of which I've never felt before.

It's me or him.

And I'm getting him before he gets me.

But I don't know how else to live. I'll never, ever escape him. I keep coming back and I don't know why, it's like he's got this invisible force that keeps me tied to him, no matter what he does. I'll never get away as long as he's alive, never.

But if I kill him, and get lifted, I know there's a high chance I'd get dropped to a charge of culpable homicide, because of my mental health and the abuse. That's only a few years in the jail. That won't work.

I want to go to jail forever.

I can't kill him, and just leave. I need to make a scene.

It's him or me.

And it ain't fucking me, mate.

We're on the futon in the living room, and next to us is the coffee table – on which he always keeps a big kitchen knife, and a claw hammer.

I stare at them and turn my head back around. And I go back and forth, trying to imagine it.

But what if he overpowers me?

So, I get up, and after walking through to the kitchen as quietly as possible, I close the door, and fill the kettle up.

I'm going to throw this boiling water over him, cut his throat, and with the knife in one hand and the hammer in the other, annihilate the cunt.

And when I'm done, he's getting fucking dismembered, and his body parts thrown out the fucking window.

I want him to suffer, I want his remains to be desecrated. I want to go to prison forever.

I just want to escape him.

I don't want to do something like this, but there's no other way.

At least in jail I'll get a script, and 3 meals a day. It's like a wee community in there, I'll be *sound*.

I just need to escape, but I can't unless I do something of this magnitude.

I know I sound psychotic, but nobody understands. Nobody understands what it's like to have someone that's meant to love you wake you up in the morning with a boot to the stomach. Nobody understands what it's like. Everyone tells me it's my fault because I'm loud.

So, fuck them all, I'll go to jail forever and live my days out there!!!

And the kettle clicks.

I open the kitchen door, and see Molly sitting there, right at his side, looking at me.

It's like she knows.

I silently point for her to come into the kitchen, and she refuses.

I creep over to the side and grab her collar. I'm trying to pull her into the kitchen, I don't want her seeing this. She's just an innocent dog.

But she digs her claws into the carpet.

And it hits me, it really fucking hits me.

I need to get out of here.

Look at what I'm about to do.

I can't.

I just need to make a plan.

CHAPTER 45

I've been talking to mum again, going down to see her every week.

It's weird because whenever I visit hers, I'm welcomed in with open arms, have my dinner made, allowed free reign over her cigarettes. But the second I move back, it's like a gigantic problem has moved into her home.

This is the only thing stopping me from asking her outright to come "home".

But the abuse is getting really fucking bad now.

It's the 21st of January 2014, and Steff hasn't long been put on a Drug Testing and Treatment Order over the Christmas and New Year period. So, right now we haven't really got a heroin habit, or he would go to prison when he attends his monthly review at the sheriff court.

But he still expects us to go out shoplifting... for fucking weed.

I'm getting sick of it.

As I leave my mums to go back to our flat, my heart sinks. I don't want to go back to him. I feel like a child that's having a great time at the park and doesn't want to leave.

The 26 bus takes me from Prestonpans back into Edinburgh, and the walk to the flat feels like I'm walking Death Row.

Getting in, and sitting down next to Steff, he asks me if I got any money.

"What? No, I didn't ask..."

He snaps, "So you've been away ALL day and didny bother askin for a lend!?"

I instincetively begin apologising, as he bounces up from the couch and starts putting his trainers on, getting ready to go out for a shoplift.

All of this over weed?

It was never just the fucking Heroin!!!

As he puts his backpack on, he spins around in front of me, grabs a handful of my hair, and drags me off the couch.

He kicks me in the chin and drops me.

I'm getting out of here.

Seriously.

I'm leaving.

This is fucking it.

CHAPTER 46

I lie there on the floor, and listen as he opens the front door, slamming it closed behind him as he storms out.

The second the front door is closed, I jump up and lock it. If he were to walk back in in the next couple of minutes, I'd get a full-blown kicking.

I can't stop shaking, my entire body is vibrating furiously, as I run around the flat in a panic.

Suitcase!!!

Unzipping my suitcase on the floor, I begin emptying drawers of my clothes into it. I'm literally ripping the drawers out of the unit, tipping them upside down over the suitcase. Fuck packing neatly, now is not the time.

As soon as the suitcase is zipped back up, I make my way out of the flat.

I can't carry this down all of these stairs, I need to take the lift.

Pressing the button, and watching the numbers above the elevator moving from G up to 1, then 2, then 3, then 4, there's about a million scenarios running through my brain. I have a feeling when these lift doors open at the bottom, he will be standing there.

The lift doors open, and I pull my suitcase inside.

I can't believe I'm fucking doing this. I've actually got a big smile on my face.

Because I KNOW I'm never coming back.

Smiling, I turn around, and notice the mirror. So I pull out my cheap blackvberry, and take a selfie.

And I upload that selfie to Facebook.

"Goodbyeeeee fucker =)"

Dear Bella,

I never went back. That was the day I left for good. A few months after I left, his next girlfriend died in his bed.

With regards to the murder, I contacted Crimestoppers anonymously 3 times and told them what I knew. But I kept my mouth shut for so long because he had me convinced that I would be killed if I say anything.

It's still sitting as unsolved.

I don't know if Steff was telling the truth about what actually happened in the house, but part of me believes it. And I held it onto my conscious for so long that phoning crimestoppers was a relief. It upsets me to see it sitting as unsolved.

I know parts of this you probably didn't want to read, in fact I think it'll be hard for most people to read, but this shit happened. It all happened, and I've lived with it for so, so long. Writing this has gotten it out.

Things have changed from starting the book, to sitting now writing the end and editing. I'm sorry things have worked out the way they have.

Bella... I'm sorry this family is fucked.

I love you

Mum

xxxxxxxxxxxxxx

ACKNOWLEDGEMENT

Firstly I want to thank myself for putting up and also dishing out a load of shite whilst I've been writing this book.

But really, I want to thank my husband William for putting up with my nonsense, encouraging me to do what I want to do with my life, but mainly for just being there when I've needed you most. You are my family and always were, I just didn't know it.

And my best friend Claire, thank you for as always, putting up with my voice notes. If it weren't for you believing me with all of this shite then I don't think I would've gotten the confidence to speak up, ever!

And my beautiful wee Bella-Caledonia, thank you for being you. Everything I do is for you.

Everyone that reads my stuff - thank you! Really, from the bottom of my heart, thank you. You reading my stuff makes these books possible.

And as usual, all the assholes, ha-ha-ha-ha.

Ria Greig x

Printed in Great Britain
by Amazon

19255908R00078